Music and Maiden Overs

**The Vic Lewis Swing String Quartet,
1935**

Music and Maiden Overs

My Showbusiness Life

Vic Lewis *with Tony Barrow*

Chatto & Windus, London

Published in 1987 by
Chatto & Windus Ltd
30 Bedford Square
London WC1B 3RP

British Library Cataloguing in Publication Data

Lewis, Vic
    Music and maiden overs: my showbusiness life.
    1. Lewis, Vic   2. Jazz musicians—
England—Biography
    I. Title   II. Barrow, Tony
    785.42′092′4   ML419.L4/

ISBN 0-7011-3142-X

Photoset by Rowland Phototypesetting Ltd
Bury St Edmunds, Suffolk
Printed by Butler & Tanner Ltd
Frome, Somerset

Contents

To Bobby Hackett, Stan Kenton and Ken Thorne
for making my musical life;
Everton Weekes, Sir Frank Worrell and Sir Garfield Sobers
for making my cricket life so memorable;
Nat King Cole for being the finest artist to work with;
to my very best friend, David Garson, and
my very best secretary, Dee Birchmore, for being there
when they were needed during crucial periods of my
show-business life; and, finally, my mother, who
supported me in everything I ever wanted to do

Illustrations

Prologue

Mayhem in Manila

The Beatles and Imelda Marcos

DURING MY LIFE as a jazz musician and bandleader in the forties and fifties, and as a show-business agent and artists' manager in the sixties and seventies, I landed in my fair share of strange situations. But in the brief midsixties period when I represented the Beatles, things got particularly hairy.

In 1966, I was working with Brian Epstein, the young manager of the Beatles. It became my responsibility to set up some of the group's biggest ever concert dates around the world, including the Far East, during the final months before the Beatles retired from touring.

In Tokyo, the Beatles did five shows at the Nippon-Budokan hall. In 1966, no other pop stars had played there. Outraged that the Beatles had been permitted to perform in the Budokan, a venue traditionally reserved for serious martial-arts tournaments and other national sporting events, the city's militant faction of right-wing students had threatened to kill the Beatles if the concerts went ahead. Tokyo's meticulous security services took the threat very seriously throughout our short stay in Japan. I formed the impression that if John, Paul, George or Ringo had been fatally wounded on Japanese soil, the security people would have been more distressed by their own failure to cope than by the death of a Beatle.

Brian Epstein asked me to travel ahead of the main party to our next destination. In Manila, our local concert promoter, Ramon Ramos, boss of an outfit named Cavalcade International Productions, told me that one quarter of the entire local police force had been detailed for Beatles duty between Sunday and Tuesday. Ramos said he expected a crowd of over 35,000 to attend the Monday afternoon performance in Manila's huge Rizal National Memorial Football Stadium. He thought 45,000 would pack into the place for the second and final concert at 8.30 the same evening. If those figures proved correct, it would be the greatest number of fans that had watched the Beatles in live performance on one day.

On Sunday 3 July, as Ramon had predicted, an enormous crowd of Filipino fans invaded Manila's international airport, and local radio and TV reporters poured

Beatles painting watercolours in the Tokyo Hilton, 1966

out a ceaseless flow of information about the progress of the Beatles' flight from Japan.

The Manila arrival went smoothly. I had arranged with the chief immigration officer and with customs, police and health authorities that the plane bringing the Beatles from Tokyo would taxi to the farthest outskirts of the airstrip immediately after landing. Here, hidden behind shrubbery, we had our limousines and a ladder to let the Beatles climb down from the aircraft before it turned round and took the rest of the flight's passengers to the airport-terminal buildings in the usual way. At the foot of the steps, Filipino officials carried out all the essential formalities of stamping passports, checking health certificates and clearing whatever items of hand baggage the four boys carried with them. The Beatles were waved through to a waiting convoy of cars and we drove off from the Cathay Pacific aircraft with an escort of six police motorcyclists.

The Beatles at their press conference in Manila, 1966

As we sped through relatively uncongested side streets and back roads to the city centre, the Beatles seemed genuinely grateful for the smart timing of the airport operation. We had dodged the fans and, besides, in 1966, their comings and goings were under increasingly close scrutiny by the drug squads of every continent and they feared the consequences of a search.

When our cars crossed intersections with the wider urban roads, we caught glimpses of a carnival procession. The brightly painted jeeps which are common-place vehicles of public transport in Manila, the colourful carnival costumes and decorated floats fascinated the four normally blasé Beatles.

Soon we were at the navy headquarters for the group's formal press conference. Although the reporters and photographers were curious to know why this unusual setting had been chosen instead of the Manila Hotel, we kept them unaware of the true reason. The secret plan was to put up the Beatles and their closest aides on a luxuriously fitted yacht for the night while the rest of our touring party checked into the hotel. After an hour with the press, the four Beatles were led from the conference room and through a rear door to a waiting launch. This ferried them to the yacht, the property of a local newspaper owner who also happened to be a friend of our promoter, Ramon Ramos.

On the yacht there was a chance of the four boys enjoying a bit of peace and privacy during their 48-hour stay in the Philippines. Hotels were never truly secure from fans and the press. With the cooperation of naval authorities, I had laid on a ship-to-shore telephone so that I could remain in round-the-clock contact with Brian and the boys. The landing the next afternoon at around two o'clock would be at a secluded point along the coast.

A few hours later, I had a message that a man from the navy was waiting to talk to me in the hotel lobby. Brian Epstein was asking me to get back to him on the ship-to-shore phone. When the link-up had been made, my first words of greeting were drenched in a torrent of abuse from Brian.

'We're not staying one minute longer on this bloody boat, Vic. It's going up and down! The boys are fed up. There's absolutely nothing to do and we want to come ashore at once. We don't want to spend any more time on this ghastly little yacht!'

I was a little taken aback, but I was used to Epstein's temper. With some difficulty, room was arranged for everyone at the Manila Hotel.

What angered me most was the gradually emerging evidence that only Brian himself found the idea of staying on the yacht unsatisfactory. In separate conversations later, both John and Paul confirmed this. And Tony Barrow, who had been on board the boat with the boys, told me their only cause for concern had been the initial delay in the arrival of their personal baggage from the airport. Two members of the group were waiting for a smoke and feared that their marijuana might have been confiscated by customs officials.

Quite early the following morning, I jumped out of bed in response to a loud knocking on the door of my hotel room. Outside stood a pair of high-ranking military officers, a general and an admiral, dressed immaculately in uniform and wearing ceremonial medals.

The visitors saluted smartly and spoke in good American. 'We're the reception committee from the Malacanang Palace. We're here to represent President Marcos and the first lady.' They said they had come to make final arrangements for our trip to the palace, where the Beatles would be presented to the president's wife and her luncheon guests. Two hundred children had also been invited.

I knew nothing of a palace lunch party with Mrs Marcos and had to say so. The boys would have remained on the yacht until two that afternoon if the original plan had been in force. The Cavalcade timetable for the afternoon suggested that the Beatles might 'call in on the first lady' at 3 p.m. and, 'from the palace, proceed directly to the stadium for the first concert'. In the general confusion of changing all the overnight accommodation, Ramon Ramos had not raised the matter of a palace visit with anyone and I had no reason to believe the Beatles were expected there.

I was, however, aware of the absolute power wielded by President Ferdinand Marcos. A request from the first family, particularly from the strikingly beautiful Imelda, was a presidential command which a Filipino subject would ignore or refuse at his peril. If Ramon Ramos had received such a request, there was no way he would have dared to turn it down. His response could only have been 'yes' or 'I'll see'. He would have had to hope that Brian Epstein could persuade the Beatles to attend. I never met Ramon Ramos again so I do not know what led up to the arrival of those officers at my bedroom door.

I explained to them that the day's plans had been laid and that timing was of the essence. Safety and security were key factors, but I would inform Brian of the request.

My visitors chilled visibly and audibly. 'This is not a request. We have our orders. The children of the aristocracy who wish to meet the Beatles will assemble at eleven.'

After a hurried wash, I threw on a shirt and trousers for a confrontation with Brian. I had to warn him, 'These people are hot-blooded. I think a snub to the president and his first lady could be unwise.'

Brian was unyielding. 'I'm not going to ask the Beatles about this. Go back and tell the generals we're not coming.'

Peter Brown, Brian's close associate, supported Brian in our increasingly heated argument. Had they agreed to make the Beatles properly aware of all the circumstances, the consequences of ignoring the palace event could have been avoided. Our convoy of cars from the hotel to the football ground could have been rerouted via the palace and the length of the Beatles' visit there reduced to a polite minimum. But my plea for caution in a tricky situation went unheeded. Epstein informed the generals very pompously that he knew of no formal invitation and he would not wake up the four boys until it was time to prepare for the afternoon concert.

That evening a special television news report showed intimate friends of the first family and their children lining up with a crowd of Manila's upper crust in a palace reception room for a meeting with the Beatles.

'The children began to arrive at ten,' claimed the TV newscaster. 'They waited until after two. At first, we were told that a mob at the yacht basin was delaying the scheduled arrival of the Beatles. Then we learned that the group was not even aboard. At noon the first lady decided properly and wisely not to wait any longer. "The children have all the time in the world, but we are busy people," she said. The place cards for the Beatles at the lunch table were removed.' The commentator concluded, 'This was the most noteworthy East-West mix-up in Manila for many years.'

Hostility towards the Beatles escalated alarmingly. In a last-minute effort to reverse the deteriorating public opinion of them, their PR man Tony Barrow persuaded Brian Epstein to read a statement of apology on a later TV news bulletin. In the filmed interview, Epstein explained that neither he nor the group had been handed any invitation. 'The first we knew of the hundreds of children waiting to meet the Beatles at the palace was when we watched television earlier this evening.' When the statement was shown, most of what Brian had to say was blotted out by unexplained interference, although the sound quality was fine for the rest of the programme.

At the end of the second concert, our police escort back to the hotel had been withdrawn and gates were locked against our convoy. This left our stationary cars at the mercy of organised troublemakers, hundreds rather than dozens, pressing menacingly against the windows, screaming insults at the Beatles and rocking the vehicles to and fro.

It was a relief to reach the safety of my room in the Manila Hotel. I warned the four boys to lock their doors and I did the same. An hour later, a police deputation arrived and commanded me to accompany them to Manila police headquarters.

'Am I under arrest?' I asked.

'We wish to ask some questions.'

I feared for my safety and made what arrangements I could to ensure that the British embassy heard what was happening to me. I have no clear memory of the journey that followed. I was far too nervous to notice anything.

I was led into an interview room and positioned in front of a large desk. I could only see the back of a man's head above the swivel chair behind the desk. I felt sure his face would show him to be Peter Lorre.

After a long silence, Lorre swung the chair to face me and snapped out two questions, 'Why did the Beatles fail to visit the first lady at the presidential palace today? Why did you snub our country?'

As variations on the same theme followed, I could only repeat the simple truth of the matter. 'I had no knowledge of the invitation in advance. Only the Beatles' manager, Brian Epstein, could have made the visit happen at such short notice.'

They ignored my references to Epstein and insisted that I was the only responsible person in the situation. 'You represent the Beatles. You did not bring them to the palace today.'

The pointlessly repetitive interrogation continued for at least three hours. It was almost dawn when I was driven back to the hotel. The 100-degree mid-summer temperature and the intensity of the verbal inquisition I had been exposed to had combined to bring me to the brink of mental exhaustion. I lay alone on my bed for several restless hours, curiously afraid to seek aid or companionship, yet unable to fall asleep.

Just after eight that morning, my bedroom door was pounded again by persistent fists. I groaned at the thought of the whole nightmare repeating itself. But the man in the corridor didn't look at all ferocious. He was a podgy little chap in a shiny suit, carrying a brown briefcase.

'Here is your bill for the income tax due on the Beatles' fee.'

Our contract with Cavalcade International Productions was very precise on the matter of local taxes. The responsibility for payment belonged with the promoters. Ramon Ramos was contractually liable for the settlement of any tax bills.

It was like talking to a brick wall. 'Your fee is taxed as earnings regardless of any other contracts.'

Grudgingly, Brian Epstein agreed to see the taxman while I began to deal with the day's new problems. Hotel staff were refusing to handle our bags. We were increasingly isolated. In the hotel lobby, I caught sight of the front-page headline carried by the *Manila Daily Mirror*: PAY FIRST – LEAVE LATER! Our tax collector appeared to have the power of the press behind him this morning.

Our baggage lorry driver seemed to be the last adult in Manila loyal to the Beatles' cause. Tony Barrow and I joined the group's roadies in the job of humping everybody's suitcases and equipment out into the street.

When all was loaded I told Brian what we were doing. I reminded him that Ramon Ramos could only hand over our fee when the tax situation had been sorted out. 'Brian, make sure you collect the money, won't you? Tony and I will go ahead to the airport and check in the whole party with KLM. When it's safe and KLM give me the OK, I'll ring you and the Beatles can leave the hotel.'

At Manila airport the concourse was totally deserted. The atmosphere was scary, as if a bomb was due to go off. As we drew up to unload our lorry, a lone cop appeared from nowhere and told us to move on.

The airport manager had ordered that the Beatles be left to fend for themselves. Even the escalators had been shut down. When Tony and I entered the departure hall with the party's flight tickets, there was not a soul in sight except for a pair of receptionists behind the KLM desk. They agreed that everything possible would be done to delay the flight's departure until the Beatles joined us, but the final decision lay with the captain.

I decided to see the captain personally and a stewardess took me out to the plane. As we reached the tarmac, I was horrified to find an enormous crowd, most of them in a hostile mood, many threatening violence and brandishing pistols in my direction as soon as I emerged from the terminal building. I did not fancy the chances of the Beatles, without police protection, getting through to the aircraft unhurt.

The pilot was helpful and promised to wait as long as possible in the hope that the crowd would disperse.

I phoned Brian. 'Leave now, go directly to the KLM desk when you get here, and have each passport ready for inspection. I'll meet you and tell you what we must do next.'

When the Beatles arrived, KLM officials did what they could for us but there was no alternative but to run the gauntlet of the angry mob between the building and the aircraft. I was the last to go, behind the rest of the party. I held a hand across my back in the hope that it would protect my spine from bullets.

A roadie, Mal Evans, was tripped by the mob and staggered on with blood streaming down one leg. Brian Epstein was punched in the face and kicked in the groin. Between us all, we shielded John, Paul, George and Ringo.

The jeering and jostling continued as we hauled ourselves up the staircase and into the aircraft's cabin. Even then our ordeal was not over. A command crackled through the cabin loudspeakers. 'Mr Tony Barrow and Mr Malcolm Evans must return to the departure building, please.'

'They're going to take it out on us,' muttered Tony. Mal asked someone to contact his wife.

Inside the terminal, Evans and Barrow were told they could not leave because there was no documentary evidence that they had arrived. Somehow their papers had not been processed with the rest when they left the incoming flight from Tokyo with the Beatles at the far end of the airfield.

It was now well over forty minutes past our four o'clock departure time. I went up to the captain's cabin with a fresh plea that we should wait while officials prepared the paperwork to bring in and usher out the last two members of our party.

Our party sat in silence, hoping to see Barrow and Evans reappear at the cabin door. I walked over to Brian and asked him quietly if he had resolved the tax problem and received the concert money. He shouted, 'Is that all you can think about? Bloody money at a time like this?' This was sheer hypocrisy on Epstein's part, of course.

As soon as our missing pair of colleagues returned, the KLM plane rose from the runway and we broke into spontaneous applause.

After this experience in Manila, no wonder John, Paul, George and Ringo refused all future offers of concert trips, regardless of the money they might have made.

First Innings

From Brent to Greenwich Village

Shearing, Hackett, Condon and company

ACCORDING TO THE story handed down over the years, a member of my family once killed a man for calling him a 'dirty Jew'.

My great-grandfather on my mother's side was a City publican in the Minories, just behind the Tower of London. At that time, it was uncommon for Jews to be the victims of any sort of social persecution, casual or organised, and the number of Jewish families resident in this country was relatively small.

One day, more than a century ago, his son, Aaron Morris, was serving behind the bar when a brawny customer with a few beers under his belt became abusive. The troublemaker wasn't a regular. If you ran an East End pub in those days, a verbal brawl or two across the counter was all in a night's work. It was when this stranger's attack took a sudden and violent anti-Semitic turn that Aaron's anger could not be contained any longer.

He jumped over the bar and fists began to fly. I doubt if it was intended to be a fight to the death but, by the time the final blows had been exchanged, Aaron's burly opponent lay lifeless on the floor.

'Blimey, he's killed the young bruiser,' muttered one of Aaron's regulars, as the crowd drew back.

It must be some measure of the unusually high respect in which the Morris family was held by the Minories community that Aaron was not even arrested on that evening, let alone charged with murder. On the contrary, his swift escape from justice took place with the connivance of the local constabulary. 'You'd better catch the night boat, son,' the police told him, and Aaron fled to Australia, never to be seen again by the rest of the family.

Along with this tale, successive generations of the Morris family have handed down a treasured document which records the award of the freedom of the City of London to my great-grandfather. This remains in my possession today.

To be a Jew in London today, well over one hundred years on, is not without its special stresses, but the particular religious pressures upon me in my early childhood were substantially more complicated. As a result of Spanish cross-pollination within the family, I was sent to La Sageste Convent where, although I was totally enamoured with the reverend mother, I realised that the burning of incense and the constant ringing of prayer bells were not for me. My curious position led me to spend an unusual amount of time considering the whole matter of religious faith and personal beliefs. I reached the conclusion that, if there was a God, he would be for all people, blacks, whites, Jews, Protestants, Hindus, Catholics, the lot. I could not bring myself to believe in a God who appeared to discriminate rather than embrace the human race as a whole. If God was not good enough for everyone, he was not good enough at all.

I decided that I was more of an agnostic than an atheist. I accepted the probability that an almighty power existed but I found it impossible to imagine God as the keeper of a little punishment book. I feel much the same today. I cannot bring myself to believe in a God capable of intervention in human affairs yet willing to observe the horrors of contemporary war without preventing further repetition of such pointless and widespread slaughter and suffering. Maybe the Power will have the last say and we shall all be blown to smithereens along with the planet Earth.

I was born in Brent on 29 July 1919, and we lived at 6 St Mary's Road. The last railway station on the local line from London was at Golders Green. Brent was rural rather than suburban territory. My show-business career has led me to criss-cross the globe many times, yet I think I would be totally lost if I was forced to live out the rest of my years too far from the Finchley Road. My home now is at Totteridge Park with my wife, Jill, and our daughter, Danielle.

The Lewis family came to Britain from France in the middle of the sixteenth century. I believe 'Lewis' is derived from 'Louis'. The Lewis line of business was antique jewellery and my grandfather's main business premises were located in Covent Garden at Cranbourn Street. The closest connection he had with the world of entertainment was via the clientele that was attracted to his Mayfair shop in New Bond Street. Here he sold superb pieces of antique jewellery to the music-hall stars of the late Victorian era, from Vesta Tilley and Gertie Gitana to George Edwards and Marie Lloyd.

Grandfather took a cue from some of his more colourful customers and turned into a bit of a playboy himself. Most of the time he was quite discreet and careful about covering his tracks, particularly over intimate affairs of the heart.

He was a very active man well into his eighties. Soon after his eightieth birthday, he announced his intention to become an entertainment-business entrepreneur by buying the Golders Green Hippodrome, more recently used by the BBC as a television studio, and the local Ionic cinema. He demonstrated his new love for the cinema by spending five or six evenings a week down at the Ionic, often seeing the same programme of silent films over and over again.

Eventually one of the family, my aunt Millie, became suspicious of this obsessive interest in the cinema and followed Grandfather to the Ionic. Yes, he really did go into the place. And no, he was not escorting any secret lady friend. Or so it seemed until Aunt Millie went in after him. There was my grandfather sitting in the back row of the stalls with a pretty little usherette. In the interval, he handed her chocolates and silk stockings. Once the lights went down, he couldn't wait to start canoodling with all the gusto of a teenager. It is my fervent hope that I shall be capable of displaying such admirable zest for life when I reach my eighties.

This is not the only trait with which my energetic grandfather kindly endowed me. As a very small boy I visited his home on the Finchley Road at Golders Green each Saturday or Sunday to collect my weekly sixpence, a traditional pocket-money bonus which I considered well worth the short trip. If I arrived early, Grandfather would still be in the bathroom. He took great pride in his appearance, grooming himself immaculately every day and allowing himself the additional weekend luxury of three-hour stints in the bathroom. I must have admired him for this and cherished a lifelong desire to do the same thing. I loathed the overcrowded communal facilities of my wartime days in the RAF and I commandeer the Lewis household bathroom for whole mornings at a time whenever Jill and Danielle give me half the chance.

By contrast, my father, Bert Lewis, appeared to be made in a very different mould. In his younger days, I believe he had been something of a rake, keeping a

The Charing Cross Cricket Club, 1904:
Vic's father, front row, centre

secret countryside hideaway down at Amersham. It was not a side he showed the family. My mother, Mayre, found him to be a very devoted and adoring husband. He was never unduly strict with me or my elder brother, Laddie. But my father's greatest love in life was cricket.

His passionate feeling for the game was indirectly responsible for keeping him out of the firing line in the First World War. At the outbreak of hostilities in 1914, he joined the Royal Naval Air Service. His commanding officers soon found out about their athletic new recruit's prowess on the cricket field – Father had already distinguished himself with Kent Second XI. Instead of finding himself on perilous airborne missions, he was kept within easy reach of Lord's cricket ground to bolster up the interservices team.

Undoubtedly, my own fondness for cricket stemmed from watching my father play with Larwood, Voce, Freeman, Patsy Hendren, J. W. Hearne and the rest. My brother and I held bats or balls in our hands while other infants stared at their rattles or sucked their dummies. One memorable day, I sat with my mother at the nursery end within talking distance of the great Don Bradman. Even when my love of music

Vic with cricket bat in the back garden of 24 Oakfields Road, London N W 11, c. 1929

took over as the main influence in my young life, cricket remained a permanent interest, one which was seldom far from my thoughts, least of all at test-match time.

My father was a very slow left-arm spin bowler. In garden games with us boys, he'd have us out with just about every delivery. He was given several presentation balls for his bowling, each with a little plaque to record the occasion and the feat. His best achievement was nine wickets for twenty-four runs (more than five wickets is generally considered pretty good).

On the other hand, Father had little to offer me in the way of musical incentive. At Christmas he would take up a one-string violin, the like of which I have not seen in many a year, and give us a solo performance of Elgar's 'Salute d'Amour'.

Apart from this annual experience, all my music came to me from my mother's side of the family. Her grandfather, Joe Daniels, was a London music publisher, a composer and an outstanding banjo player who performed with the Ethiopian Harmonists minstrel jazz group during the 1880s. Her father, Nip, eldest of a family of no fewer than sixteen boys and girls, played the banjo and the bones and was a tap dancer. Nip and three of his brothers became music teachers at Oxford and Cambridge. I still possess a magnificent old banjo which Prince Edward, later King Edward VII, presented to Nip.

My earliest musical memories are of summer months spent at the home of my uncle Dan in Southsea. My mother took me there for long holidays from the time I learned to walk and talk. Uncle Dan was a professor of music and leader of a minstrel group known as the Scarlet Mysteries. The furniture of his front room was dominated by an upright piano which had a variety of banjos and guitars spread around its feet. As soon as he finished giving a music lesson and the room was free, I would wander in and take my pick of the instruments. Uncle Dan encouraged me to play the four-string banjo. Later, I stayed with the four-string format when I took up tenor-guitar playing.

Throughout my life, I have possessed unusual stamina as a guitarist, able to play rhythm guitar hour after hour without my right arm becoming intolerably tired. I put this down to a teenage football accident which happened when I was at Clark College, Finchley.

The captain of the college team, Alec Reeve, never saw eye to eye with me but the atmosphere of continuous enmity between us intensified when I began to take out a girl he had fancied for some time. I might have known he would take his revenge on the football field. Although I was a mere five foot four and weighed only seven stone, Reeve put me in goal for a match where we faced hefty opponents.

At the beginning of the game, I stared in horror at the team of older and bigger boys emerging from the visitors' changing room. But, as a sportsman, I knew the captain's orders must be followed and I took up my goal keeper's position. Midway through the match, a member of the other team sent a fast ball flying towards the right-hand side of the goal mouth. In a desperate bid to stop them scoring, I took off with both feet so that I sprang at least half a metre into the air. Before I could complete the heroic save, a muscular body collided forcefully with my abdomen, sending me spinning head over heels. I must have blacked out momentarily. When I opened my eyes, I was staring up from the ground into a mass of smiling, sweaty faces belonging to my team mates. Someone asked facetiously, 'What shall we pick up first, his right arm or the rest of his body?'

The sports master ordered me off to the doctor's, where my arm was put in a splint and bound up. As he tied off the bandages he told me, 'You'll have to go to Hendon Cottage Hospital for X-rays in the morning. It's too late to catch them now before the department closes.'

My mother was taking afternoon tea with my aunt Millie when she spotted me approaching the front door, head bowed miserably and splint straps all around my neck. They plied me with cups of hot sweet tea before putting me to bed. The next day, the X-rays were taken and I was sent back to my own doctor's surgery.

'Grip my hand as hard as you can now, boy,' commanded the doctor. Without additional warning, he twisted my arm through an alarming number of degrees. As I paled with agony and bit my lip, he explained calmly, 'We need to break the bone again so that I can reset it for you in the proper position. Then you can have your plaster put on and the arm should mend nicely.'

The resetting job was a washout. To this day I am unable to put my right arm straight out in front of me. The unexpected bonus is that I find it easier to play the guitar. The bias of that injured arm towards my body allows it to rest comfortably on a guitar belly and a long session is far less tiring. Therefore, when I remember with gratitude the encouragement and advice that came from Uncle Dan during all those summers I spent in Southsea, I have to couple this with a word of thanks to Alec Reeve, whose dirty trick backfired.

When I was about ten years old and on a vacation visit to Uncle Dan's, I had my earliest experience of flying. One day, my cousin Clara took me on a trip to Portsmouth where they were advertising fifteen-minute joy rides over the Isle of Wight from the local airstrip in a ramshackle four-seater plane. When we landed, Clara stood by quite unsympathetically while one green-faced little boy scuttled off to be sick. This unhappy initiation failed to put me off flying. In my time, I must have travelled at least 4 million miles by air and my collection of Concorde flight certificates increases annually.

The majority of my intercontinental jet flights were made for business reasons, but I have managed to link the more recent jaunts with a favourite hobby – stamp collecting. I know some people who say that philately will get you nowhere, but I decided to devote a part of my own stamp collection to Concorde. I addressed an envelope to myself and tucked it in my briefcase at the outset of each Concorde trip. At Heathrow, before the flight, I took my envelope to the airport post office, where I bought stamps for it, first-day issues if any happened to be available, and got the clerk to hand-cancel them on the spot so that the franking stamper would indicate clearly the airport name, the date and the hour. During the flight, the Concorde pilot would sign my envelope to verify my flight number and destination. On arrival, I bought a second set of stamps to stick on the reverse side of my envelope and got it franked by hand again by the local post-office staff to show where and at what time my journey had been completed. In this way I have assembled a set of envelopes which is unique – a matter of significance in the world of philately.

• • •

Apart from the lessons learned in Uncle Dan's front room, my main source of musical input during childhood was the wireless. I remember the family owning a primitive old crystal set in the twenties and I spent happy hours trying to locate as many different music programmes as possible. Even at that age, I hungered for different sounds, everything from jazz to the classics. Two contrasting pieces impressed me particularly – something called 'Street Scene' and the love section of Tchaikovsky's *Romeo and Juliet*.

I associate my earliest experience of listening to music on gramophone records with visits to stay with a cousin named Nigel who lived at the Ship Hotel in Hove and owned a small but fascinating set of Parlophone records in the old rhythm style. When I started my own collection, the very first recordings I bought included 'Walking The Dog' by Eddie Lang's Orchestra and Jimmy Dorsey's 'Praying The Blues'. My earliest idols were Eddie Condon and Eddie Lang.

Eddie Condon was born near Chicago and became a banjo-playing guitarist in the earliest days of American white-dominated jazz. The typical new Chicago-style jazz groups were small and used trombone, clarinet and trumpet. Condon became known for playing a four-string guitar.

Meanwhile, in New York, Paul Whiteman's forty-piece symphonic concert orchestra was playing syncopated big-band music, things like 'Rhapsody In Blue'. Whiteman's orchestra included some intriguing names – the cornet player Bix Beiderbecke, the guitarist Eddie Lang, the violin player Joe Venuti. Splinter groups were set up as singers and musicians left Whiteman's line-up. One of Whiteman's singers, a member of his Rhythm Boys group, was Bing Crosby. When Crosby left to start a solo career, he took the Whiteman guitarist, Eddie Lang, with him. Not long afterwards, Eddie Lang joined Joe Venuti to form a most unusual quartet. Their combination of violin and guitar sounds fascinated me. It was quite different from most of the jazz being played in Britain at the time.

By 1935, I was approaching my sixteenth birthday and the time had come to decide what to do with my adult life. My schooling had been rather chequered. I suffered from bronchial infections as a youngster, and my parents were persuaded that I would be better off beside the seaside than in London. The result was that I spent the best (or worst) part of three years breathing the beneficial ozone on a particularly muddy stretch of the Essex coastline. My health showed some improvement but my progress in the classroom was not helped by all this chopping and changing. In any case, even if I did not yet admit it openly to myself or others, I was heading for some sort of job as a professional musician. I wanted to make jazz music of my own.

Among my friends at this time were a guitarist named Alan Haymes, Ronnie Burton, who was a violin player, and a cousin, Joe Muslin, who was taking lessons on the bass. In 1935, I invited them to join me when I formed my first official group, the Vic Lewis Swing String Quartet. This group was totally influenced by the Venuti and Lang team.

Although he had come under the same family influences, my brother was never a serious candidate for a place in the Quartet. He played, but was insufficiently ambitious about his music to do much with it. At one time he ran a band with Joe Kunz, son of Charlie, the popular pianist, but the venture never really got off the ground and they stuck to doing local gigs, mostly in the ballroom above the Orpheum cinema at Temple Fortune.

Meanwhile, the Vic Lewis Swing String Quartet auditioned successfully for Carroll Levis, then famous as the radio *Discoveries* man. He ran talent-contest shows which introduced newcomers, mostly raw beginners who appeared at heats he held in local theatres before graduating to radio. Levis arranged our first radio work, including a broadcast for the BBC. Shows for Radio Luxembourg followed from the Leicester Square Theatre, and a tour of theatres in the London area. We started with a show at the New Cross Empire. This was our first sniff of the greasepaint. Two musicians joined us: Phil Pearce, who played the trombone, and a remarkable pianist named Ray Leizer. We called ourselves the Blue Swingers when we grew from quartet to sextet size by bringing in Leizer and Pearce to broaden the band's musical scope.

Vic with the Stéphane Grappelli Quintet at Bates Club, Mayfair, 1945. The singer is Edna Kaye, the bass player Tommy Bromley

Backstage at the Paramount Theater, New York. Back row: Rafael Mendez, Ray Leizer, unidentified, Kai Winding; front row: Harold Davison, Mel Torme, Sam Donahue, Vic Lewis

Picture given to Vic by Django Reinhardt after Vic had taught him how to sign it

Leizer stayed with us for a couple of years and then took his family to live in South Africa. This amazing man had the guts to volunteer for wartime military service in Israel, where both his arms were blown off. I came across him again in 1950, taking part in a New York radio show. There was Ray, playing the piano as wonderfully as ever, having taught himself all over again, using two artificial limbs.

Surprisingly fast, we found ourselves mingling with legendary giants of the international jazz scene: at a pub in Wood Green, I remember playing with the Belgian gypsy guitarist Django Reinhardt and the violinist Stéphane Grappelli. In the years leading up to the Second World War, I came into contact with an increasing number of notable jazzmen, many joining in our various jam sessions, particularly at the Orange Tree, Friern Barnet, a favourite place run by a pair of ardent jazz fans. During this period I met Carlo Krahmer, a blind drummer who played with a London-based big band made up entirely of blind school students. The pianist with that band was George Shearing, who later played piano for me when Ray Leizer left for South Africa. Krahmer was impressed with the way I played guitar when he came to hear us at the Orange Tree. Together, we formed our own group with Reg Arnold, a brilliant young cornet player.

My association with Krahmer and Shearing turned out to be most fruitful. In the centre of London, a few small recording studios had sprung up. At a cost of less than one pound, it was possible to make an acetate recording of the band in one of these places. In the absence of modern tape-recording facilities, they were a boon and did a roaring trade among musicians. We must have made over forty records in this way. The title that stands out in my mind today, five decades later, is 'Stooge Blues', done in 1938 and featuring a terrific performance by George Shearing.

We managed to persuade just about every new musician who showed the slightest sign of promise to join in these sessions. We had George Chisholm, Leslie 'Jiver' Hutchinson, Bertie King, Johnny Clays and many more. Chisholm is recognised even today as one of the greatest trombone players Britain has ever produced. He came from Scotland and was gigging in London by 1938, ending up in the RAF during the war like most of us. Jiver played trumpet, came from the West Indies, and had been in London for about five years when I met him. He and Bertie King, who played alto and tenor sax and clarinet, joined Ken 'Snakehips' Johnson's London band, playing at the famous Kit Kat Club. Clays was a large fellow who played trumpet, a gigster around England. Some would remain on the professional jazz scene for their entire working life while others disappeared to faraway places. At the last count, Johnny Clays was driving a taxi in New Zealand.

With so many exciting developments, I decided to hire myself a press agent. The man I chose was Felix Mendelsohn, who led a double life in those days, acting as a publicist but also successfully fronting his distinctive Hawaiian Serenaders. One afternoon, Felix phoned me and said, 'I've come across an extremely interesting new girl with a rather special singing voice. I'd like you to hear her. I think you might want her to join your band.'

I arranged a rehearsal at the Regal Ballroom in Cricklewood so that we could audition this new discovery. After several numbers, I made up my mind that she was not for us. I told Felix, 'She's far too straight. Her voice has no jazz feeling. She'd be no good at all to me.' The lady's name was Vera Lynn.

For a short spell, I steered myself away from the jazz scene. I accepted the offer of a tiny acting role as a school prefect in the film *Goodbye, Mr Chips*, starring Robert Donat and Greer Garson. I had to be up before five o'clock each morning to begin the two-hour journey to Denham Studios. When I got there, the film people would make me up, fit me with a top hat and dress me in the rest of the old-fashioned sixth former's gear. One morning they told me the scenes we were to shoot would involve a pupils' paper chase through the woods and I was handed some flimsy running shorts and a singlet. This was the final straw. No wonder there are not too many musicians who also make the grade as movie stars! I hurried back to the band, putting all visions of Hollywood stardom out of my mind for ever.

My future involvement in the making of motion pictures revolved around the soundtrack side, although I did act just once more. This was in March 1948 when I donned shorts, again; to play an army sergeant in Egypt for the Terry-Thomas and Jean Carson film *Date with a Dream*. For this production I also wrote all the tunes.

•　　•　　•

In 1938, I made my first trip to America, not a normal adventure for a nineteen-year-old boy in those days. It was an educational adventure which my father paid for when I persuaded my parents that my burning ambition was to make a career as a jazz musician. My mother was specific – 'You must go to America to learn your craft.'

Through playing with my band at the No. 1 Rhythm Club in London, I had formed a firm friendship with Leonard Feather, a jazz journalist who ran the club. By now, Feather was in New York. I cabled him with my arrival details before setting sail on the *Queen Mary*. Early on a warm October morning, I watched the Statue of Liberty loom larger as we headed for port after almost five stormy days at sea. I recognised the place at once as my spiritual home. This was America, Land of Jazz!

I took a taxi to the Taft Hotel, just off Broadway, and my first phone call was to Leonard Feather. He had been busy on my behalf. I would be able to sit in with the Joe Marsala group that very night if I turned up with my guitar at the Hickory House around ten o'clock.

Marsala played clarinet, a type near enough to the Chicago style. At this time, his small jazz group was rated among the top half-dozen similar outfits in New York. He had played with Eddie Condon, hence his influence, but he also had his wife, Adele Girard, playing harp with his group, which gave it a distinctive sound.

What was more, if I caught the subway to Greenwich Village after that, there was every chance I'd meet two of my greatest idols, Eddie Condon and Bobby Hackett, one of the finest cornet and trumpet players in the jazz world.

I filled in time wandering around New York's record stores like a wide-eyed child, gaping in utter delight at the wares on show in the brilliantly lit windows of Milt Gabler's Commodore Music Shop, until it was time to head for the first of the night spots that Leonard Feather had listed for me.

At the Hickory House, I found the band perched high above the main bar, sitting in a circle on a fairly small stage. I reached over and shook hands with Joe Marsala. Leonard Feather had paved the way perfectly. Marsala grinned, probably amused at my youthful eagerness, and said, 'We've been expecting you, Vic. Come up over the bar as soon as you're ready.' I undid my guitar case and proudly joined the jazzmen on stage. The next minute, I was playing there beside Joe and his brother, Marty, with Joe Bushkin on piano, Artie Bernstein on bass and Buddy Rich on drums. This boy from Brent was in his heaven.

Much later that night, I followed Leonard Feather's further directions and found myself standing on a deserted Greenwich Village sidewalk outside a rather unimposing building. This was a club called Nick's and I had not come to the wrong place. It seemed a colourless setting for what I expected to be an exciting encounter but, once inside, I realised that this was a magnificent musical environment. I jammed with Bobby Hackett's band, which was run jointly by Hackett and Eddie Condon. At dawn, I returned to my hotel a happy man, having become friendly with both of them. And all on my very first night in New York.

Hackett and Condon told me I was welcome to play with them at Nick's as often as I wanted for as long as I liked. Prevailing exchange restrictions prevented them from talking money but they offered me all the food and liquor I required. In any case, the real reward came in the form of lessons learned and experience notched up in the company of my peers. For six wonderful weeks I spent my nights playing not only with the Hackett line-up, which consisted of, among others, Pee Wee Russell, George Wettling, Brad Gowans and Dave Bowman, but also with the relief band, led by Sidney Bechet. This was an all-black group which included Zutty Singleton, Wellman Braud and Danny Baker. On other occasions I sat in with such stars as Tommy Dorsey, Jack Teagarden and Louis Armstrong. As a kid, I had never imagined I would even see these people perform.

Joe Marsala joined me on one of the recording sessions I managed to do while I was in town. Most of the other guys from Nick's also agreed to come into the studios with me, all playing for nothing, of course, so that I would be able to take home vivid audio memories of my visit on acetate. (In 1986, when the original recordings were almost fifty years old and the surfaces of some acetates had become a little scratchy, Esquire Records in London reissued a set of these historic New York tracks in album form. The compilation is called *Vic Lewis and his American Jazzmen*.)

On reflection, I must admit I was unduly narrow-minded over music in 1938. I would blot out just about everything that did not classify as Chicago-style jazz. In spite of this, I could not resist accepting Tommy Dorsey's invitation to hear his big band while I was in New York, and a number of his best-known musicians became

**Bobby Hackett, Pee Wee Russell and
Vic Lewis, holding each other's
instruments**

The Tommy Dorsey Clambake Seven
(Johnny Mince on clarinet, far right),
New York, 1938

Lester Young and Vic outside the
Famous Door nightclub on 52nd
Street, New York, 1938

my close friends. Among them were Moe Zudcoff, better known in later years as the bandleader Buddy Morrow, and Johnny Mince, a man I was to meet again during the war and remain in touch with to this day. Mince is still in his sixties, reckoned to be one of the best clarinet men in his particular style. He can play big-band style (Dorsey/Goodman/Shaw) or in the more traditional jazz style. In either case, his technique is flawless.

In New York, it took me a little while to grow accustomed to the intriguing fact that it was quite possible to stroll the streets casually and come face to face with not only one but several top musicians at a time. On an aimless walk down 52nd Street one afternoon, I bumped into Lester Young, the tenor player. He introduced me to his bandleader, Count Basie, saying, 'This young guy is from England and loves jazz.'

Bill Basie said, 'We're about to rehearse, Vic. Why don't you come in with us and sit on the piano stool next to me?' Ten minutes later I was sitting there beside the remarkably friendly Count Basie, close to Lester Young, Herschell Evans and a rhythm section made up of Freddy Green, Walter Page and Joe Jones.

Until that day, only small-group jazz had interested me. The experience of sitting there with Basie's men broadened my musical outlook in a single afternoon. In the long term, the lasting influence of Basie and his band on my own expansion as a musician and my future direction as a bandleader in the forties and fifties proved to be considerable.

The memory of another outstanding band, which I saw at the legendary Roseland Ballroom, remains vivid. This was led by Bunny Berigan, his first big band after he left Tommy Dorsey's orchestra. I was honoured to meet the great man and join him for drinks when he took a break. Later, Joe Bushkin and Buddy Rich became part of his remarkable line-up. Sadly, Bunny died relatively young, like many of his talented contemporaries, but, for a while, he surely ranked among the finest jazzmen of a memorable era.

My experiences during that stay in New York were not restricted to music. When I was playing at Nick's, a lady, maybe in her late twenties and rather drunk, said she liked the way I spoke and was I from England? She was quite friendly and plied me with drinks in my breaks. I must have told her where I was staying, for back at the hotel I had a phone call. She was in the lobby and I told her to come right up.

I let in this half-stupefied but rather attractive lady, and she began to take her clothes off. When we were just getting into bed, I was horrified to hear a knock on my door. I immediately thought of all the films where people were set up in similar circumstances and either had their throat cut or were held to ransom. I feared I was going to die. 'Who is it?' I enquired in a shaky voice.

'This is the house detective and your door is unlocked.'

After getting out, thanking him and locking the door, getting back into bed against this woman's body was too much. Hence my first encounter was a failure. Needless to say, I made up for it in the years to come.

By bus I set out from New York to explore the land of jazz and stayed a while in Memphis, Tennessee, and in New Orleans. I sat in with various groups and I listened to church revivalist singers.

One Sunday morning in Memphis I believed I was dead. I had not realised that the room where the church choir were starting their service with a hymn was right next door to mine. Coming out of sleep, I could hear angelic voices. It was a great awakening.

Via St Louis and Indianapolis, I returned to New York and picked up where I left off, playing at Nick's and meeting the greats. When I had to return to London, two kind people took a young English jazz unknown to the boat. They stayed with me on the *Queen Mary* until it was time to leave. They were Zutty and Marge Singleton, both long gone but never forgotten.

Sergeant Vic Lewis
meets Major Glenn Miller

RAF days and the Radio Rhythm Club Sextet

DROVES OF LONDON musicians used to gather every Monday morning in Archer Street, close to Piccadilly Circus, to see what new jobs were going for the week. On my first day back in town, acetates of the New York sessions clutched proudly under my arm, I was treated as a bit of a hero by the Archer Street crowd and spent most of the morning recounting my adventures to each fresh arrival. I also picked up a job, a six-week engagement in Antwerp. My partner was to be a pianist named André who did not know a single word of English.

We overcame the language barriers, although our earliest dialogue consisted almost entirely of song titles as we put together our nightly programme. 'Blue Skies,' I would mutter. 'The Man I Love,' he would reply. We both loved jazz and spoke the same music.

We were playing in an exclusive Antwerp night club where the men were accompanied by some of the prettiest whores I have ever seen. It was not until the end of my stint at the club that I found out the truth about the big-spending male clientele. They were Nazis, the vanguard of the German invasion of Belgium only a matter of months later. I declined an offer to remain after my initial contract ran out. Clearly, it was time to go home.

My parents had purchased a house at Hove a few years earlier to serve as a summer place and weekend retreat. During the last few months before the outbreak of World War II, I deserted the London music scene to take temporary work as a farm labourer in Sussex. This was an unsettled time for many people; few of us felt we could predict which way the tide was going to turn. There was no reliable information, only a lot of dreadful rumours about what was going on in Germany. An atmosphere of unreality mingled with confusion and fear hung over our everyday lives, although, in typically British fashion, we went about our normal business and hoped things would work out for the best.

One day in September 1939, I was on my way to visit my girlfriend Georgina, who lived about 10 miles from my parents' place. I remember turning into the narrow country lane where she lived just as the distant sound of sirens signalled the official outbreak of war. Had someone set off the warning in error? Perhaps they were practising. I stamped my foot down hard on the accelerator and drove to Georgina's front gate. As I ran up the path and through the open door, I saw her family gathered beside the radio with grim faces and I knew there had been no mistake.

I was handed a whole tumbler filled with whisky and downed the stuff in one great gulp, unaware that the idea had been to pass it around the room. At any other time, we would have had a good laugh about that.

I received my call-up papers during the third week of September. I had volunteered for service with the Royal Air Force. Within hours of reporting for duty at Uxbridge, I had (a) lost most of my hair, snipped off by the most barbaric and least competent barber since the demonic Sweeney Todd, (b) been issued with a uniform clearly made to measure for Quasimodo rather than for V. Lewis, and (c) landed in bed with vaccine fever, having been jabbed full of evil juices by witch doctors who swore I was now protected against everything from cholera to tetanus. Soon I was ordered from my sickbed to red-ochre the kitchen floor in the officers' mess.

Until September 1939 I had never been called upon to clean my own shoes or make my own bed, let alone attend to kitchen floors on bended knee. Of course, worse was to come. Square bashing, for example. This was a period of sheer hell designed to teach a new recruit how to salute his superiors, fire guns and obey the most absurd order without question. They told me I would remember only the good times. There were good times? I do remember, even half a century later, marching a number of miles to Uxbridge railway station, en route for Cardington, with 400 other unfortunates, each carrying a hefty kit bag which looked at least as tall as my five feet seven inches and felt as heavy as my seven stone. To be accurate, one muscular recruit carried two bags, and one little airman, named Lewis, carried none!

At Cardington, the hut I called home was located no more than 100 yards from a hangar once used by the ill-fated R-101 airship. A few years earlier, the family had watched from the back garden as that remarkable craft went floating by above our heads on its maiden flight. For no particular reason, I had remarked to my parents that night, 'I bet this is the first and last time we see the 101.' The airship crashed only hours later.

From Cardington we were packed off to Yatesbury, a godforsaken air base situated six miles from Calne, right in the middle of the Wiltshire Cotswolds. Here I was to train as an air gunner wireless operator. I proceeded with vigour to learn the Morse code and found that all it did was give me a headache, and I wondered how I could be so musical and yet not accept the dots and dashes that came from my earphones.

During the winter of 1939, our camp was hit by an epidemic of meningitis. Men were falling dead from their beds. This is a highly contagious disease and the conditions at Yatesbury seemed to increase the dangers of infection. The huts were inadequately heated and, because of the severe winter weather, seldom ventilated. Panic set in among the airmen. We may have been trained to march across squares and sling rifles around but the majority of us were still ordinary civilians in uniform, quite unready to act with military discipline in such a situation.

Deputations were made to the commanding officer but nothing was done and more victims fell ill daily. Several of us determined that drastic measures were called for. Our action committee included Johnny Stewart, later to become a leading producer of light entertainment programmes for BBC Television, and a jazz trombone player, Bobby Mickleborough, who was the camp bugler. The decision was made to organise a mass march-out: we would refuse to return to our quarters until the outbreak of meningitis was quelled and proper precautions adopted. The first task was to inform every airman on the base of what was happening. I was chosen for the mission because I could go from hut to hut with my guitar and spread the word while appearing to be there to entertain the boys.

Several thousand of us marched out through the gates a few days later. By order of their CO or otherwise, the guards did nothing to stop the mass departure. Across fields and along roads covered in deeply drifted snow, we trudged to Calne station and took trains to our various homes. When the weather improved and recovering patients confirmed that the epidemic was over, we went back to Yatesbury. A group of senior officers met our trains but we were not placed under arrest, as many had feared. Instead, we were given a decent meal, supplied by the dear ladies of the Women's Voluntary Service, and sent to the town hall where overnight sleeping accommodation had been prepared. No official disciplinary action was taken when we returned to the camp, although we had committed what amounted to the extremely serious crime of going absent without leave in wartime.

Perhaps the most surprising aspect of this story is that the Air Force and the War Office suppressed all information about the incident and the news media failed to get wind of it. To the best of my knowledge, I am publishing the details here for the first time.

My personal punishment for being among the ringleaders was to be posted as a guard on Christmas Day. I had to protect a massive water tower, perched on a hill two miles from the camp, by standing beside it with my gun all day long. The group captain turned up in person that morning, commanding me to order arms while he peered through the barrel of my rifle to see if it was clean. Then his sidekick dished out Christmas lunch, including a Lyons individual fruit pie in a box with a holly design printed on its lid. I threw mine over the hill.

The following spring, the camp chaplain invited me to put together a variety show. Over a period of weeks, a makeshift stage was constructed in the canteen. I was amazed at the range of show-business skills to be found among the men. I produced a company which included jugglers, a magician, an orchestra and a front line of chorus girls, Yatesbury being one of the first bases to receive an intake from the Women's Auxiliary Air Force. Our opening performance played to a packed house. While the majority of the camp's off-duty inhabitants were in the canteen watching our show, a German aircraft swooped from overhead and shot up the camp. On any other evening, hundreds of us in our huts would have been sitting targets for the enemy's attack. As it happened, not a soul was hurt.

One weekend, on 48-hour leave, I broke my leg climbing the garden wall and spent the next month hobbling around Hove on crutches. My witty father derived much joy from spreading the word that his younger son had been shot down dramatically over the English Channel during a highly dangerous RAF mission. The moment he led me into just about any pub between Hove and Brighton, drinks were on the house for the poor injured hero until I felt forced to admit the embarrassing truth.

When I returned to Yatesbury, I discovered that my entire squadron had been posted to Normandy in my absence. And every colleague on my air gunner's course was dead. Every man jack had been wiped out in a single German attack.

I failed my wireless test and was posted to Brampton, headquarters of Bomber Command's training wing. I was met at Huntingdon station by a Flight Lieutenant Grayson who told me, 'I'm your commanding officer. Actually we're the only two chaps here at present. We are RAF Brampton, Headquarters No. 7 Group!'

He took me to a private house, where I was to be billeted, and explained our job. 'Over a thousand men are due in here soon. We have to find homes for the lot of them. It means going round the district, accompanied by the village bobby, interviewing suitable householders until we have enough beds for everybody.'

I found that the citizens of this charming little place became substantially more public-spirited over the whole idea of putting up Bomber Command personnel when I told them it would mean double food rations all round plus seventeen shillings per head per week. I took the opportunity of moving myself into the local butcher's house. Apart from enhancing my general dining prospects, this provided me with the chance to cadge the occasional joint or leg of lamb to take home to my parents at weekends.

After one weekend off, I arrived on the base at breakfast time and was told that every available man was to be rounded up at once, with rifles drawn. 'A German parachutist has landed and he has to be taken alive.'

Four hundred of us made our way stealthily to a copse where we were ordered to fan out into a full circle and surround the area. We were told not to load our rifles yet but, being scared stiff, we put in the ammunition anyway. Gradually, we marched towards the pinnacle where we hoped to capture our German without bloodshed.

In fact, it was a false alarm. The 'parachutist' turned out to be one of our own comrades, a keep-fit fanatic who was resting there in the long grass after his daily run. He made a curious sight, standing there in his little white shorts and vest, blinking in the early morning sunlight, arms raised obediently above his head while our officers verified his identity. If he had been an enemy and shooting had started, our own people would have stood every chance of fatally wounding one another at fairly close quarters since every rifle being aimed at the centre of that circle also pointed directly at a fellow British airman.

While I was stationed at RAF Brampton, a guitarist named Sid Gross asked if I would do a gig on string bass at the Rex, nearby in Cambridge. When I reached the bandstand at the Rex, I was introduced to a young drummer named Jack Parnell, and a shy-looking pianist, Ken Thorne. Ken and I struck up a firm friendship that very evening, although it was quite a while before our paths crossed for a second time.

In 1942, my next posting took me to Winslow in Buckinghamshire. By this time, I was a fully fledged sergeant, having refused the chance of going for a commission. For me, becoming an officer entailed too many trappings.

My commanding officer made the amazing decision to put me in charge of the police. In neither physique nor mentality have I ever borne the slightest resemblance to a policeman, so this was typically in keeping with the eccentricities of the wartime Air Force.

At about two o'clock one morning, I was guarding the headquarters with my corporal and half a dozen airmen when a shot rang out. I was convinced the Luftwaffe had landed and immediately blew my whistle, the alarm used at night to alert all posts around the base. Then I rushed to the main gate to make sure all was secure. There I found the source of the false alarm. The guard I had placed at the entrance had fallen asleep with his fingers gripping the trigger of his rifle. When something startled him, he had fired the gun and shot his toe off. This brought my duty with the police to an abrupt end and resulted in a posting to greener pastures.

For most of the final three years of World War II, I was stationed at Bomber Command HQ, High Wycombe. This time, instead of handing me the responsibility for a security section, the commanding officer, knowing my background, gave me a bunch of musicians. I was told, 'There's this band of some sort being posted to us. Do what you can with them, sergeant.' The new arrivals turned out to be the Buddy Featherstonehaugh Quintet, comprising Buddy on tenor sax and clarinet, Don Macaffer on trombone, Harry Rayner at the piano, Frank Clark on bass and Jack Parnell playing drums.

I joined them and, in due course, we became the Radio Rhythm Club Sextet. We landed a series of weekly BBC broadcasts, taking the place of Harry Parry. This involved official permission to take a fair bit of time off from our other duties and make regular trips into the West End of London. Our BBC shows were done at either the Paris Studios in Lower Regent Street or the Aeolian Hall in Bond Street. In addition, we did numerous broadcasts for the forces' radio network from the Fortune Theatre in Drury Lane.

Problems of priority arose when, as well as spending an increasing amount of time with the Sextet, I was made NCO in charge of discipline and poison-gas protection, a curious combination of responsibilities for a jazzman. I was already supervising all the catering requirements for the sergeants' mess, ordering the

**The Buddy Featherstonehaugh group,
RAF, during the war**

booze and looking after the WAAF girls (in all sorts of ways). On days when we did our radio work, we would drive out of camp at the crack of dawn, often returning late at night. The pressures were building up. The crunch came one lunchtime when I was doing a stock check behind the bar and someone thumped on the closed serving hatch. A voice boomed out, 'This is the station warrant officer and I want a large whisky at once.'

I replied, 'It's two o'clock. The bar is shut. Go away!'

He flung open the hatch and screamed, 'The whisky, sergeant! Now! And give me a good splash of soda!'

I don't know what came over me. But I do know what came all over the station warrant officer – a good splash of soda, straight from the syphon, all over his fat red face and all down his neatly pressed blue uniform.

As I stood there, paralysed momentarily by the sheer enormity of my reckless action, I knew I had to move fast. I threw down the empty syphon and rushed to the sick bay where I passed out in a heap on the floor. There was no pretence about my collapse, and a nervous breakdown, brought on by exhaustion as a result of overwork, was diagnosed. I was sent off to Buxton Hospital. But for the break-down, I would have been stripped of my rank and deported to RAF Hades for my serious misuse of a senior NCO.

While I underwent psychiatric treatment at Buxton, I came into close contact with some of the war's most terrifying casualties. In the next bed to me was a sergeant pilot who had been shot down over the English Channel after a bombing expedition. His entire crew had been killed. When they dragged him from the sea, barely alive, the poor chap had insisted on contacting his home to assure his family that he was safe. When the phone call went through, his doctors had a fresh piece of tragic news for the pilot: his wife and his children had died in an air raid.

When they returned me to High Wycombe, with a clean bill of mental health, I was put in charge of the bunker where all the local planning for Allied air raids of Germany took place. It was here that Bomber Harris and all the top brass deliberated with the chiefs of the United States Air Force, sorting out how many serviceable planes each nation still had at its disposal from day to day and how these might be deployed to maximum military advantage. I was privy to top-secret talks concerning many crucial moves in the final stages of the war: for instance, I heard the exact details of the D-Day invasion long before the event.

One day we were told there was to be a major training manoeuvre between our mob and the Black Watch division of the Army. This would take place not far from our High Wycombe base. Apart from using blanks instead of live ammunition, we were to act exactly as if this was the real thing.

A group of us, including my colleagues in the Buddy Featherstonehaugh band, had to occupy a small village four miles from Knapp Hill. The Black Watch had threatened to capture some poor Bomber Command NCO and send him back home smothered in tar and feathers, not part of the official battle plans, so I took the day's manoeuvring seriously, despite the general apathy and indifference among my squad of musicians. When I heard sporadic fire, I ordered my men to crawl on their stomachs to avoid being seen above a low wall in front of us. Buddy Featherstonhaugh rebelled at this, stood up and flung down his rifle. 'I'm not staying down there on the bloody floor. I don't like playing soldiers.'

I showed him the colour of my three stripes. 'It's an order! Lie down!' With a yelled obscenity in my direction, Buddy set off on his own. As he sauntered past a gap in the wall, an enemy bayonet lunged out and pierced his cheek. Buddy didn't have to play soldiers any more that day. He spent the rest of an uncomfortable week in sick quarters, the side of his face scarred by jagged lines of stitches.

During the summer of 1944, we played for a special dance in the officers' mess. The function was scheduled to finish around midnight but, at that hour, a distinguished air commodore approached Buddy on the stand and asked if we would mind playing on for a short time. 'There'll be a few extra bob in it for you and your boys and I'd like to buy you a round of drinks. We'd appreciate it if you stayed an extra fifteen or twenty minutes.' He could not have been more civilised about it and there was no question of turning the informal request into an official order.

Grudgingly, Buddy agreed and we played several more numbers. Then the air commodore came over again. Maybe he was going to thank us, maybe he was going to ask us to keep playing. Before anything had been said, Buddy came out with a string of oaths and obscenities which were bound to make the officers' ladies cringe. The very next morning the band was posted and the Radio Rhythm Club Sextet came to an end.

Despite the total union ban on performances by foreign musicians in Britain during and long after the war years, Americans were allowed to come over here as part of military bands. In this guise, a vast array of talented American jazz artists visited our shores during the middle and later years of World War II, when the number of shows put on for the troops reached a peak.

In 1943 and 1944, the Americans brought a spectacular stage production called *This Is the Army* to the London Palladium. The whole company, including the pit orchestra, was made up of servicemen. To my great delight, the musicians included my good friend Johnny Mince from the Tommy Dorsey band. Along with Jake Koven and Joe Gudice, Mince joined me on a number of memorable jam sessions while the show was in town. We even found the time to make some private recordings together.

Jake Koven played Chicago trumpet in the Bobby Hackett style which I love so much. He went back to America after the war and played with New York session bands. Joe Gudice played tenor sax and clarinet. In 1945, when he was in bed with his wife, a ceiling collapsed, crushing his back so badly that he was paralysed for the rest of his life. He died in the mid-1980s.

We became such a close group that the Americans stayed with my mother at her home in Oakfields Road, Temple Fortune. My father had died in 1941, at the age of only fifty-six, from peritonitis. Eventually, after the worst of the German air raids appeared to be over, my mother had moved back to London. In 1943, it was easy to pick up property in and around the capital very cheaply, since many Londoners had left the Home Counties when the bombing began. My brother and his wife bought a new place for themselves, close to Mother in Oakfields Road.

After the Palladium show, the next bunch of Americans to turn up in London came over here with the US Navy. They were led by Sam Donahue, one of the best tenor-sax players in America, and included Johnny Best, a former Glenn Miller band member who became a good friend. With these boys I made a number of private recordings and took part in the making of some BBC discs for the forces overseas.

As a rule, the BBC began their 'International Jazz' sessions somewhere after midnight and, regardless of London air raids, we played on until dawn and later. Some of the very finest American and British jazz musicians got together for these historic performances, which would never have taken place but for the war. For one session, I remember bringing in the great violinist Stéphane Grappelli as a guest and writing a piece called 'Tricolour Blues' to mark the occasion.

Another American visitor who appeared on the London jazz scene around that time was a marvellous trumpet player named Jimmy McPartland, over here with the US Pioneer Corps. He married a piano player from Sussex, and Marian McPartland has since become a great lady of jazz in America.

Of all the transatlantic bands we were privileged to hear in Britain during the war, one of the most welcome was that led by Glenn Miller. As Captain Miller, later promoted to major, he brought over his remarkable Army Air Force Band and we did many broadcasts together in London. On one occasion, we played with the Miller band at an annual charity event called Jazz Jamboree, at the Stoll Theatre, Kingsway. Miller had a tremendous line-up. One of his musicians was Carmen Mastren, another friend of mine from the Dorsey band. During a break in the show, I was chatting over old times with Carmen when Miller's authoritative voice boomed out over the public address system. 'Mastren! Get on the stand!' That was the way Glenn Miller treated his men.

The darker side of Miller's nature displayed itself again at the end of that Jazz Jamboree show when he introduced some of his best-known musicians, people like Mel Powell and Peanuts Hucko. When he came to his drummer, Miller announced, 'This is a former bandleader in his own right, Ray McKinley.'

McKinley did a little drum break in light-hearted recognition of the applause his introduction drew.

**Vic with Glenn Miller at the Jazz
Jamboree, London, 1944**

'You can cut that out, McKinley! You can do that stuff with your own band but not while you're playing for me.'

There was a gasp of disbelief from the 2500 people in the packed auditorium. I wish I could say that the man had been smiling when he said it, but, unfortunately, Miller was never renowned for the possession of a sense of humour. He was a stickler for strict military discipline even when he was rehearsing for a radio show in the privacy of a BBC studio. The band had to be in place long before Miller was scheduled to arrive. As the bandleader walked in, all his musicians would be called to attention by Broderick Crawford and every man had to spring to his feet.

This evidence, coupled with other remarks I heard him make, left me with the firm impression that the true-life Glenn Miller was a far cry from the beloved Mr Nice Guy for whom cinemagoers shed tears a decade later when James Stewart starred in the bandleader's sugar-coated screen biography. The truth is that few tears were shed when the news of Glenn Miller's disappearance reached the band in France.

Many conflicting stories circulated among his former associates when Miller went missing in December 1944. One insider told me Glenn had refused to fly to Paris with his band, insisting that he should travel in grander style.

The story went that Miller was out on a binge with a pilot friend the night before he was due to cross to the Continent. Seemingly, he persuaded this pal to fly him to Paris on his own. Not having recovered from their boozing session, the pilot took off in the wrong direction, heading west instead of east, carrying Miller far out over the Atlantic. When their fuel supply ran out, the aircraft would have been lost at sea, many miles from the Channel area where search parties looked in vain for wreckage. This was related to me in confidence by an insider at the time, and never mentioned in public until now. If it is true, this version of what happened certainly explains some of the mysteries that have always surrounded Glenn Miller's tragic disappearance.

•　　•　　•

During my six years in the Royal Air Force with Bomber Command, I played some cricket, but not consistently. On one occasion I was asked if I would like a game against a team visiting us from Upper Heyford, a Bomber officers' training unit station. Their side was captained by none other than Flight Lieutenant Bill Edrich. Bill became one of the finest batsmen England or Middlesex ever had. Later, he and Dennis Compton were known as the Terrible Twins. They were among the few people ever to score over 3000 runs in a year, an almost impossible achievement.

As the number of games I played diminished, my game deteriorated. From a pretty fast bowler I degenerated to a pretty medium-paced bowler. Whereas I had been able to call up a good reserve of stamina in earlier days, I was tiring easily after, say, eight or ten overs.

•　　•　　•

After the enforced break-up of the Radio Rhythm Club Sextet, I remained at High Wycombe for a few more months before being sent to the RAF station at Bawtry, in Yorkshire. I was told by my new CO, 'Actually, this place has been shut down and I'm the only officer left on the station. Therefore, you're to act as the warrant officer in charge. It's just a matter of protecting the whole property and preventing it from being occupied by the enemy.' They provided me with an armoured car and thirty men. I placed my security forces at strategic points and drove round the seven-mile perimeter from time to time, checking that no part of the base was being occupied by enemy sheep or stray goats.

One day, my commanding officer called me into his office and said very grandly, 'I wish to review all the men this morning. Every single airman is to be on parade with rifles all clean and shining for my inspection.'

I tried to explain the flaw in this plan. The entire airfield would be left unprotected, totally unguarded against enemy occupation, while this pointless little ceremony took place.

My protests were brushed aside. 'You have your orders. Just carry them out.'

I decided I could be equally nutty. 'In that case, sir, I resign. I shall leave the Royal Air Force.'

I went to my hut, packed my gear and marched off in the direction of the main London road, intending to hitchhike my way home to Temple Fortune. Two miles down the road, a car stopped to give me a lift. The driver was my commanding officer. Quite incredibly, he drove me all the way to the A1 without a single reference to our conversation.

When I arrived home, my brother telephoned the RAF Medical Headquarters in Hallam Street to say that I had collapsed from nervous exhaustion. When he explained that this was a repetition of an earlier illness, they suggested I should be sent to the RAF hospital just down the road at Mill Hill. Here I received a new course of psychiatric treatment before being released from the service in 1945.

The Vic Lewis and Jack Parnell Jazzmen

Band on the road

Ken Thorne and Harold Davison

DURING THE HEYDAY of the Buddy Featherstonhaugh Radio Rhythm Club Sextet, the band was under contract to the HMV label, for which we made well over two dozen records. Most of this material was a million miles away from the Chicago jazz style which was always closest to my heart. After one HMV session in 1944, I collared our producer, Wally Ridley, and talked him into letting me record my kind of music. Apart from Eddie Condon, I was influenced by the soprano-sax playing of Sidney Bechet, who produced a very wide vibrato sound. The only other soprano-sax player I heard in those days was a young boy named Ronnie Chamberlain, whom I discovered in a small London club. I was hugely impressed. With Chamberlain playing soprano and alto for me, I was able to make music that fused Chicago with Bechet.

Wally told me I could cut a couple of sides for the Parlophone sister label. Jack Parnell, our drummer, said, 'What about me? Don't I get the same treatment?' It was arranged that we would do two sides each, all on the same day. I knew whom I wanted to use in the way of musicians and my plans included Jack.

When the day arrived, Jack had not fixed any musicians or otherwise prepared for his segment of the session, so we put down all four titles under our two names. That was the birth of the Vic Lewis and Jack Parnell Jazzmen.

The Vic Lewis and Jack Parnell Jazzmen were to operate between 1944 and 1946 and top the small jazz-band section of the *Melody Maker* and *Musical Express* popularity polls. We made several hit records; one of them, 'Ugly Child', sold almost 50,000 78-r.p.m. copies, a most impressive figure for a jazz record. There were no pop charts based on record sales in those days; the hit parade, based initially on the sale of sheet music, came into being in 1952.

Jack Parnell was demobbed several months after me and we decided to take the Jazzmen into variety theatres. Jack's uncle, Val Parnell, was a show-business impresario with good theatrical connections, which boded well for our joint Jazzmen venture. Then Jack's mother, Olive, came on the scene. She insisted that her son was too much of a star to share a dressing room with the rest of the band.

Before the end of our first engagement, Jack and I were summoned to a meeting at our agent's office. He told us, 'I think the band's title has to change. It's far too unwieldy as it stands. It spoils the billing.'

Jack nodded his head but avoided looking in my direction. 'This makes sense, you know. Only one of our names should be used.'

I realised at once that Jack's mother was behind all this. 'It is a bit long, isn't it? I won't mind a change at all, Jack, as long as you don't object to your name being taken off.'

I could see that Jack was embarrassed by the whole business and it became clear that the joint venture was collapsing around our heads. Asked point-blank for their opinions, the Jazzmen voted unanimously to stay with me rather than break away to be part of some fresh Jack Parnell aggregation. The outcome was that Jack chose to join the Ted Heath band and I continued to run the Vic Lewis Jazzmen.

Vic with Jack Parnell

When Parnell left the Ted Heath band, his uncle, who ran the London Palladium, got Jack the job of heading the music department at ATV. Jack is best remembered by many for his stint in charge of the pit orchestra for the long-running sixties TV variety show *Sunday Night at the London Palladium*. More recently he has looked after the music for *The Muppet Show*, and now plays with jazz groups all over the country.

After the departure of Jack Parnell and his replacement by our new drummer, Harry Singer, the Vic Lewis Jazzmen contained Reg Arnold on trumpet, Ronnie Chamberlain playing soprano and alto, Jim Wilson on trombone, Jimmy Skidmore on tenor and Johnny Quest on bass. I continued to play the guitar and our pianist was Ken Thorne. At the beginning of May 1945, our previous piano player, Dick Katz, had left and Jack Parnell had reminded me of our gig at the Rex – 'How about contacting Ken from Cambridge?' Ken Thorne was a doctor of music and a church organist. He was also a keen jazz musician, with a particular partiality for Bob Zurke from the Bob Crosby band.

The Vic Lewis Jazzmen began to broadcast a late-night programme of dance music each Friday for the BBC in Southampton while we were resident at the city's Court Royal Hotel. One evening almost a year later, when I was back for another appearance at that same hotel, this time with my freshly formed big band, a rather thin and awkward-looking man carrying a saxophone case came up to me during an interval. 'Excuse me, but do you think I could sit in and play a few numbers with the band?'

I asked him what sort of professional experience he had.

'I have played with Stan Kenton.'

To the outsider, this might sound like a marvellous recommendation, but just about every American musician who wanted to sit in with a British band after the end of the war would claim to have played with Stan Kenton, Woody Herman or Duke Ellington. It had become a standing joke among musicians. I had to be cautious.

'Perhaps it would be best if you just blew a jazz number or two with my rhythm section before you sit in with the full band.'

To my amazement, the stranger proceeded to give out with some of the finest alto-sax playing it had ever been my pleasure to hear. This will surprise few jazz-orientated readers once I reveal that our guest's name was Art Pepper. Without hesitation, I invited him to play on and to return the following night. This he did, to everyone's delight.

In January 1946, the Jazzmen became the first British group to tour abroad after the end of World War II. We began a series of Scandinavian dates in Denmark and the welcome we were given at the port of Esbjerg was little short of sensational. All the way from Odense to Copenhagen the reception was just as warm at every stop we made. Everybody handed us red and white ribbons or flowers and the whole band was hailed like a bunch of heroes. After our opening concert in Copenhagen, we were the guests of honour at a magnificent party given by Svend Asmussen, the distinguished Danish violinist.

The Vic Lewis Jazzmen perform for
BBC TV, 1947

The Vic Lewis Jazzmen leave for
Scandinavia, January 1946

At the height of the merrymaking, an outstandingly beautiful young girl approached our table and asked for my autograph. Her good looks were not typically Scandinavian. She was dark-haired and slender. To write the dedication above my signature, I needed to know her name. 'It's Inga,' she said.

'I think Inga should join us for a little drink,' I said to Svend. A schnapps or six later, the party was hotting up. Inga and I were holding hands and gazing into one another's eyes.

On the road, the Jazzmen shared twin-bedded hotel rooms and if one man got lucky and was first back, the bedroom was his for the rest of the night. Although I seemed to be getting extremely lucky with Inga, I was beaten to our room by Ken Thorne.

By now, excessive quantities of schnapps and lager were threatening to render the pair of us legless at any moment. Without having the remotest idea where Inga lived, I suggested I take her home in a taxi. We hailed one outside the hotel and Inga gave the driver elaborate directions in Danish. I was hoping she lived alone in some cosy little apartment nearby, but twenty minutes later we had driven out of the city and were heading for the outer suburbs of Copenhagen. At last we stopped and Inga explained that she lived with her mother in a one-roomed flatlet. 'You'll have to wait in the cab while I speak with my mother.'

Moments later, she came running back. 'It's OK with my mother. I have told her that you are an Englishman.' I paid off the taxi driver and quizzed her as discreetly as I could about the sleeping arrangements. She smiled and replied, 'I told you it is OK. My mother agrees to go upstairs and stay with our neighbours. We shall not be disturbed for the rest of the night.' Never had I come across such an obliging mother!

At 7.30 the following morning, I was startled into consciousness by a knock on the door. For a split second a strange sense of guilt came over me, coupled with the fear that a ferocious mother was about to march into the room and attack me with a kitchen cleaver. But Mother was all smiles. 'Good morning! Here is some coffee and pastries.'

Inga went through the belated formality of introducing me. 'Vic is a very, very big bandleader.' I was flattered. She turned to me. 'I must get up now or I shall be late. You may stay here in bed as long as you wish. It's OK with my mother.'

Inga disappeared into the bathroom while I tackled my Danish pastries and convinced myself that the past few hours had been more than just a heavenly dream. Then she returned and opened her wardrobe door. My mouth dropped open as I watched her put on her neat little school uniform and pick up a satchel full of textbooks from beneath the bed.

From Denmark, we travelled north to Sweden on the last leg of the tour. Here I forgot all about my Danish schoolgirl sweetheart in the suntanned arms of a Swedish blonde of slightly less tender years. We seemed to stay close to one another throughout the band's six-week visit and I was utterly smitten. Over a candlelit dinner on our final night, in the heat of the moment, I proposed marriage and invited her back to England.

Instead of accepting instantly, gratefully and passionately, she said it would be best for us both if I left the restaurant now, at once, and without any prolonged farewell. 'Don't look back,' she pleaded as we parted, but I could not resist a backward glance from the doorway. I could scarcely believe my eyes.

The Swedish blonde was no longer even looking in my direction. Instead, she was stretching out her arms towards another man and gazing into a new face, one that was instantly familiar to me. I watched in amazement as I saw our trombone player sliding eagerly into the seat I had just vacated. The lady had skilfully two-timed the pair of us for six weeks.

Back home in London, we discovered that the music scene had dried up quite a bit during our absence. Perhaps the time had come to rethink the band's policy. When Reg Arnold, our trumpeter, left to go on the stage as a comedian, the line-up was a little unusual and we knew we would change it before very long. Meanwhile, as a sextet, we landed a summer residency at the Exeter Hotel in Bournemouth. Bending to the sedate atmosphere of the hotel's palm court, we added a couple of Noël Coward numbers to our repertoire. Ken Thorne put together a version of 'We'll Gather Lilacs' and 'It Might As Well Be Spring' because we thought this was what would go down well with lunchtime listeners at the hotel. We also had a library of what I call 'top and tail' stuff, meaning that we played an introduction and went into the tune at the beginning, and we had an end. The rest was improvised jazz solo work in between. It was a polite form of light, swinging music, not at all my cup of tea, but the snooty ladies of Bournemouth and their chinless escorts still figured we were too jazzy.

The final years of the forties were a period of substantial musical evolution for me. I opened my ears to a wider range of styles and my mind to fresh ideas. I developed as a writer, an instrumentalist and a bandleader.

My chief mentor and increasingly good friend during this time was Ken Thorne, who came to live with my mother and me shortly after the band's split from Parnell. Ken became like a second brother to me. He brought to the Jazzmen not only his excellence as a pianist but also a knowledge of writing. His experience as a writer had been confined mainly to smaller groups but his work possessed great panache. It was through Ken's influence that I came to listen to Shostakovich and Delius. We bought sets of 12-inch HMV records, rare as gold dust at that time. I listened to the Shostakovich first and fifth symphonies and recordings of the Delius 'Song Of The High Hills', the piano and the violin concertos. This experience revolutionised my outlook on all types of music. A whole array of fresh musical possibilities became available to me as a writer and performer. I had written several études for the Jazzmen and Ken had arranged these. My first effort was 'Étude To Eileen', dedicated to the lady I was going out with at the time. I marked the end of the affair with 'Étude In Ashes'. Other pieces, all part of a series broadcast by the BBC, included 'Étude To Life' and 'Étude In Blue, Green And Red'.

During our many discussions, Ken convinced me that what we really needed was an orchestra with a larger sound. When we were building our orchestra and doing an increasing number of broadcasts, Ken's special abilities began to display themselves. I remember one evening when we needed two arrangements for a BBC broadcast the next day. At half past ten, I found Ken fast asleep on the sofa in the lounge. He brushed aside my complaints with a vague wave of his hand. 'Don't worry, Vic, the scores will be done in time. I couldn't think of anything earlier but I'm sure it'll come right by morning.' In the middle of the night, I heard Ken get up and go downstairs. At breakfast, he handed me a sheaf of music. All the parts for both arrangements were there.

A score is the complete arrangement for all the orchestra's instruments. As a rule, it is scored in concert pitch. This means a copyist is brought in to do the transposing of each part to the pitch of the appropriate instrument. The remarkable fact was that Ken had not done a score at all. He had written the parts and transposed them in his head. There are very few musicians anywhere in the world capable of working in Ken's way. His unusual talents were a boom throughout our relationship. Under his watchful eye, I attempted my own first arrangement, taking the George Gershwin song 'Soon'. It took me all of ten days to score this. Even now, I find it much easier to conduct and read than to play and read.

Big-band jazz came out of the Paul Whiteman era. When breakaway musicians from Whiteman began to play without Whiteman's vast bank of strings, some of their groups fell into the new category of swing bands. Swing bands played in a style governed by their leaders and their arrangers, the leader determining the style, the arranger adapting everything to that. Benny Goodman, Artie Shaw and Tommy Dorsey led bigger swing bands, which became known more simply as big bands.

Bands were formed to play big-band music, 'big' meaning about sixteen musicians. There would be five saxophones: two alto, two tenor and a baritone. There would be three or four trumpets and a similar number of trombones. The rest would be a rhythm section, including piano, guitar, bass and drums.

Few big-band records filtered through to the British retail market during the war years. Because the jazzmen played at various military bases, we picked up V Discs, special records issued exclusively to American service personnel at outposts around the world. Among the V Discs I was lucky enough to pick up were some of the first big-band jazz recordings by Stan Kenton and they proved to be strongly influential. Kenton was giving me loud, vehement jazz, not as swinging as he was to become but, nevertheless, strong stuff. And I was equally influenced by Boyd Raeburn's expressive use of clarinets, flutes and horns.

From this colourful mix of musical input, I put together in my head a personal impression of my ideal jazz form, influenced by symphonic music but with ad-libbed solo passages.

In November 1946, the radio debut of the Vic Lewis Orchestra received a positive reaction from the Beeb and the public alike. Much of the money to launch the big

**Vic, Ronnie Chamberlain, Dill Jones
and Harold Luff meet Benny Goodman
in London, 1949**

band was put up by a businessman named Gerry Davis, who was also a dedicated fan. Ken Thorne and I had discussed our ideas for a cooperative type of large orchestra with the remaining members of the sextet at the end of that summer. Then we rounded up extra musicians in London and threw ourselves into a strenuous ten-week rehearsal schedule. Ken wrote fresh arrangements and we had smart new band uniforms made, and a set of posh-looking music stands. The launch took the form of a special afternoon performance in Mayfair's place of the day, Gunter's Restaurant in Curzon Street. We invited all the key people from the BBC, the music business and the press.

The media thought the new band was a sensation. On the strength of our single show at Gunter's, offers of work poured in from all quarters. With Ken Thorne's highly original writing, we were offering something that differed a great deal from the music played by the majority of contemporary London bands. What we were doing sounded similar to the music of Boyd Raeburn, whose arrangements by George Handy surely must have been influenced by the same classical writers. Although I have always disliked the clarinet as a solo instrument in jazz, I am not against its use in a section for tone colour. This seemed to give the Vic Lewis Orchestra its own identity, setting us apart from the bands of, say, Ted Heath, Ambrose or Geraldo.

Our sound was modern. The Orchestra's billing read: 'The Music of Tomorrow by the Band of Today'.

The Vic Lewis Orchestra always had at least one resident singer, although I used to take some of the vocals myself. Our first vocalist was a very pretty girl named Helen Mack. Helen was a Scottish teenager who was accepted in London as one of the best recording and radio singers of the day. Before coming to me, she worked for a short spell with Nat Gonella's band. A passionate love affair began to smoulder between Helen and Ken Thorne, but Helen had a domineering mother who whisked her out of Ken's arms and away to America. She made a name for herself on the Las Vegas cabaret scene. Unfortunately, she died young.

Once the Orchestra took off and we found ourselves spending an increasing amount of time on the road, we needed a band manager to look after all our gear as we travelled. We had been rehearsing in the Conservative Club hall at Harlesden and I had noticed that the same bright-looking young lad, Sid Maurice, seemed to turn up at most of our daily sessions, watching silently while the Orchestra played and often coming up to ask me questions afterwards. This likeable 16-year-old jumped at the chance and remained my roadie for twelve years. It was with much heartbreak that I had to let him go in 1958, when the band could no longer afford even Sid's modest salary. He had little difficulty getting work elsewhere, initially as road manager with Cliff Richard and later with the Harlem Globetrotters.

Another young fan with whom I became friendly around this time was Peter Bould. I met Peter in London in 1945. He came from Morecambe, where he ran a small record shop. In the beginning, his special value to the band was that he possessed portable recording equipment, relatively rare in those days, and would come out to make amateur recordings of the band for us at various gigs. Today, Peter is a sound supervisor for Thames Television and one of my best friends.

• • •

One morning in 1947, I was telephoned at home by a stranger who wanted to know if I would be interested in doing a Sunday concert for him at Hackney Empire. He told me, 'My name is Harold Davison. I've just left the RAF and I intend to go into show business.' His decisive approach intrigued me.

We arranged to meet at the Quality Inn coffee shop in Leicester Square. Harold turned out to be a funny little man wearing a green porkpie hat. I was fascinated by his forthright style of conversation. By the time we left the Quality Inn, I had offered Harold Davison the job of managing the band and he had agreed to come and hear us in action. We walked down Coventry Street and round to Mac's Rehearsal Room, just off Archer Street.

Without further formality, our deal was concluded. Harold was to be employed in the role of the band's manager for the princely sum of £10 per week, to be reviewed after he proved himself. I made one condition: 'While you look after the Vic Lewis Orchestra, you must not book any other bands.'

Not long afterwards, Harold signed up the Tito Burns Sextet. When I tackled him about this, he was unrepentant. 'I can book Tito's group without clashing with what I do for your band. It'll be better for us in the long run.' I asked him how come, and he said, 'The more bands we have, the bigger the agency will grow.' Agency? What agency? Harold hadn't finished. 'When you find it's time to pack in the big band and retire, the agency we build up now will be a ready-made business for you, Vic.'

Clearly, it was necessary to define fresh terms for the whole setup. Reluctantly, I agreed that Harold should go ahead and put his agency idea on a proper footing. Instead of continuing to be paid a salary by me, he would start taking commission on bookings, or splitting commission with other agents. I had no intention of sharing in the business or taking any part of the commission monies Harold hoped to earn. Again, I made the firm condition that Harold should never book any band that was in competition with my own orchestra. He agreed to abide by this stipulation but I doubt if he ever had the slightest intention of doing so. I was horrified to find out within weeks of our new arrangement that Harold had taken on Teddy Foster's orchestra, an outfit of similar size to mine and one that would cause inevitable conflicts of interest over bookings.

Davison was appointed to be manager of my band, but he also arranged our bookings. We did not have an agent to do that as a separate job. Often an act has a manager and not an agent, with the manager handling the bookings personally. There is a blurred line between the two job titles: what each does often depends on individual circumstances. Davison became an agent when he signed up other bands and established himself as their booker.

**Stan Getz, Vic, Harold Davison, Trixie
Shearing, George Shearing and Don
Lamond at Bop City on Broadway, 1950**

Artie Shaw and Harold Davison, with Vic (right), 1956

Generally, a manager takes two or three times as much commission money as an agent. An agent takes 10 to 15 per cent of the earnings he generates for his client. A manager gets anything from 20 to 50 per cent. He guides an artist's career. He works closely with his client, often invests fairly substantial cash in launching and publicising an act and promoting the image, and spends considerable time and effort on the whole project.

An agent is responsible for obtaining work for the acts on his roster, often in association with a manager, who may dictate the type of jobs that are and are not acceptable and the sort of money he is after in the way of fees. If an agent finds himself representing people who have no personal management, he may well get more involved in the situation, working at close quarters, giving direct advice to his client and receiving in exchange his brief regarding the artist's aims and ambitions. Just how much of that he is prepared to get into for a flat 10 per cent is entirely up to an individual agent.

Sometimes the term 'personal manager' is used instead of 'manager'. Often this has no particular significance, although someone who is an artistic mentor rather than merely a business adviser may prefer to add the 'personal' touch.

•　　•　　•

The activities of the Vic Lewis Orchestra became broader as more people began to accept our music. One radio project brought us a headline in the *Musical Express*: VIC LEWIS TO APPEAR ON THIRD PROGRAMME. The Third was the highbrow BBC radio service where one did not expect to hear light music or bands such as ours. The booking came as a result of a friendship which Ken Thorne and I struck up with the producer Pat Dixon, while we were recording a series entitled *Listen My Children*, which proved to be popular with more avant-garde sectors of the listening public.

In each programme we featured famous guest stars and an original Ken Thorne composition. I had the pleasure of conducting an augmented orchestra consisting of over sixty musicians, including a marvellous string section, and the George Mitchell Singers.

In 1949, we were extremely proud to represent Great Britain in a prestigious international jazz festival in Paris. But as soon as we were introduced – '*Maintenant, l'orchestre de Grande Bretagne, avec leur chef d'orchestre, Veek Levis*' – booing broke out all over the hall. This was the way French jazz fans greeted any outfit from Britain. They believed that only small groups of black musicians could produce worthwhile jazz. But I think we converted a few Frenchmen to the British way of big-band jazz that night.

It was also a great opportunity to meet all those American musicians who were unable to come to England. I spent as much time as possible with people like Charlie Parker, Miles Davis and Sidney Bechet – but not the three together because, sadly, Bechet bitterly hated the more modern styles of Parker and Davis, and refused even to stay in the same hotel.

PROGRAMME DU FESTIVAL DE JAZZ 1949

(pouvant être soumis à des modifications de dernière heure)

Dimanche 8 Mai
(en soirée : 20 h. 45)
OUVERTURE DU FESTIVAL
*
SYDNEY BECHET
*
PETE JOHNSON
*
Oran « HOT LIPS » PAGE - « Big
Chief » RUSSEL MOORE DON BYAS,
GEORGE JOHNSON, etc...
*
MILES DAVIS, TAD DAMERON
Quintet,
featuring : James MOODY,
Kenny CLARKE - « bass » SPIELER
*
CHARLIE PARKER'S Quintet
featuring : Kenny DORHAM, AL. HAIG,
Tommy POTTER et Max ROACH

Lundi 9 Mai
(en soirée : 20 h. 45)
FESTIVAL BE-BOP
*
CHARLIE PARKER'S Quintet
featuring : Kenny DORHAM, AL. HAIG,
Tommy POTTER et Max ROACH
*
JACK DIÉVAL et son Quintette,
avec Bernard HULIN, Hubert FOL,
Em. SOUDIEUX et Richie FROST
*
MILES DAVIS, TAD DAMERON
Quintet,
featuring : James MOODY,
Kenny CLARKE - « bass » SPIELER
*
VIC LEWIS BOPSTERS
et ORCHESTRA

Mardi 10 Mai
(en soirée : 20 h. 45)
FESTIVAL SIDNEY BECHET
*
SYDNEY BECHET
*
CLAUDE LUTER et ses LORIENTAIS
*
PIERRE BRASLAVSKY et son Orchestre
*
Oran « HOT LIPS » PAGE - « Big
Chief » RUSSEL MOORE, etc...
*
CARLO KRAHMER et son Orchestre

Mercredi 11 Mai
(en soirée : 20 h. 45)
DE LA NOUVELLE ORLEANS...
...AU BE-BOP
SYDNEY BECHET
avec Pierre BRASLAVSKY
et son Orchestre
*
CLAUDE LUTER et ses Lorientais
*
PETE JOHNSON
*
JIMMY McPARTLAND
et CARLO KRAHMER et son Orchestre
*
Oran « HOT LIPS » PAGE - « Big
Chief » RUSSEL MOORE DON BYAS,
GEORGE JOHNSON, etc...
*
Hubert FOSTAING et son Sextette
*
MILES DAVIS, TAD DAMERON
Quintet,
featuring : James MOODY,
Kenny CLARKE - « bass » SPIELER
*
VIC LEWIS et son Orchestre

Jeudi 12 Mai
(En MATINEE : 17 h. 15)
(Réservée aux Étudiants, prix réduits)
Oran « HOT LIPS » PAGE - « Big
Chief » RUSSEL MOORE DON BYAS,
GEORGE JOHNSON, etc...
*
PETE JOHNSON
*
MILES DAVIS, TAD DAMERON
Quintet,
featuring : James MOODY,
Kenny CLARKE - « bass » SPIELER
*
Trumpet no End », avec
COLEMAN, AIMÉ BARELLI,
REX STEWART
... PAGE, ... etc...
*
... WALD Quintet
... HOLLENHAGEN

Vendredi 13 Mai
(en soirée : 20 h. 45)
SYDNEY BECHET
avec P. Braslasky et son Orchestre
*
PETE JOHNSON
*
Oran « HOT LIPS » PAGE - « Big
Chief » RUSSEL MOORE DON BYAS,
GEORGE JOHNSON, etc...
*
ARMANDO TROVAJOLI
*
Trio BERNARD PEIFFER
*
International PIANO Contest

Samedi 14 Mai
(en soirée : 20 h. 45)
CHARLIE PARKER'S Quintet
featuring : Kenny DORHAM, AL. HAIG,
Tommy POTTER et Max ROACH
*
les BOB-SHOTS
*
HAZY OSTERWALD Quintet
featuring : Ernst HOLLENHAGEN
*
TOOTS THIELSMANS' Trio
*
MILES DAVIS, TAD DAMERON
Quintet,
featuring : James MOODY,
Kenny CLARKE - « bass » SPIELER

Dimanche 15 Mai
(EN MATINEE : 17 h. 15)
SYDNEY BECHET
avec P. BRASLAVSKY et son Orchestre
*
PETE JOHNSON
*
Oran « HOT LIPS » PAGE - « Big
Chief » RUSSEL MOORE DON BYAS,
GEORGE JOHNSON, etc...
*
ALL STARS FRANÇAIS « JUNIOR ».
*
MILES DAVIS, TAD DAMERON
Quintet,
featuring : James MOODY,
Kenny CLARKE - « bass » SPIELER
*
CHARLIE PARKER'S Quintet
featuring : Kenny DORHAM, AL. HAIG,
Tommy POTTER et Max ROACH

Dimanche 15 Mai
(en soirée : 20 h. 45)
SYDNEY BECHET
avec P. BRASLAVSKY et son Orchestre
*
PETE JOHNSON

Programme du festival de jazz, 1949:
**Vic shares the bill with Charlie Parker
and Miles Davis**

We did a fair amount of touring with our big band in the final years of the forties, and became the first band to visit Holland under that country's new exchange arrangements with Britain. The occasion was marked with all due ceremony, my band awaiting the arrival of their counterparts, Holland's Skymasters, on the tarmac at Northolt Aerodrome, then London's main airport. As the Dutch plane came to a stop, we struck up the band in noisy welcome, before boarding the same aircraft for its return flight. Our own airport reception in Holland was staggering. Hundreds of boys and girls in traditional Dutch costume brought gifts of gin and Edam cheese and took us to the Bols factory itself for a grand and boozy tour of the place.

At the culmination of our three-week stay, I was invited to appear in Amsterdam's Concertgebouw, Holland's foremost hall of music, where I conducted the massed bands of the Ramblers, the Skymasters and the Vic Lewis Orchestra playing Stan Kenton's 'Intermission Riff'.

I enjoyed grand functions, but it was often a single musician's exceptional artistry that made me feel I had chosen the right line of business by becoming a bandleader. Among the outstanding people who played for me in the forties was Kathleen Stobart, one of the finest tenor-saxophone exponents I ever heard. Kathy was always on the move, staying with us for a while and then going away to form her own groups. She had a strong influence on the band and through working for us she met her second husband, a great trumpet player, Bert Courtley.

Another lady who made a lasting impression upon me during that period was not a musician at all but the sexy young girlfriend of our drummer, Peter Coleman. Diana Fluck came from Peter's home town of Swindon. She turned up to most of our band rehearsals while she was with him, and her looks and manner took the mind of many a red-blooded musician off his job. We were sorry when Peter's relationship with her came to an end and Diana changed her surname to Dors and sauntered off to be a film star.

Rehearsal, c. 1949: Vince Bovil (tenor sax), Ronnie Chamberlain (lead alto sax), Johnny Shakespeare (lead trumpet), Gordon Langhorn (lead trombone), Vic, Jack Waters (trombone), Hank Shaw (trumpet), Kathy Stobart (tenor sax), Peter Coleman (drums), Stan Smith (trombone), Harold Luff (trumpet)

Our tours to Eire were memorable in their way. Even in the outlying towns, the dances did not start until at least ten o'clock at night and seldom finished before three the next morning. I think the men wanted to make sure they allowed themselves maximum drinking time in the local pub before their womenfolk dragged them off for a dance. Often we found ourselves playing in quite remote villages for crowds consisting almost entirely of farmers and their families. They made unlikely audiences for our style of progressive jazz and I was convinced we would be lynched at any moment or ordered to play Irish jigs and reels. Our compromise was to give them a very grandiose arrangement of 'The Soldier Song', Eire's national anthem, to open each performance. This brought every patriotic Patrick in the hall to his feet and the band could do no wrong for the rest of the night.

In some places, the entertainment included a beauty contest and I had to perform the perilous job of acting as a judge. On my way into the hall, I would be waylaid by muscular relatives of competitors who threatened me with physical ill-treatment unless their daughter or cousin or girlfriend won. I was usually taken out the back door or escorted by the Garda.

However, this was not the case in Drogheda, where the moment I saw this most beautiful Irish girl I did not have to think twice about who was going to win. In fact, neither did anybody else. I really was overwhelmed by her beauty, and on crowning her Miss Drogheda, I asked if I might see her after the dance.

To say one falls in love at first glance must be true. I could not wait for the dance to finish. When at last we met I asked her if she would come back to my hotel for a drink. Knowing the upbringing of most Irish girls, I thought this was going to be difficult, but we talked and talked through the night. I told her how much I had fallen in love with her, and somehow she felt the same way about me. When the morning came and she saw us off at the tour bus, we had carefully made plans to meet outside Dury's Hotel in Dublin at a given time on the Saturday week.

The day we arrived in Dublin, I rushed around to Dury's and was horrified to learn that all the transport had gone on strike in Eire that day. There was no way she could get down to Dublin. She did not know where I was staying, I did not have her address, and phones were not in use at that time in the average home. This was the heartbreaking end to a romance that I am sure would have blossomed.

•   •   •

Stuff the BBC!

Jill and Music for Moderns

ALTHOUGH OUR LIFE in the late forties centred on the tremendous amount of work we put in to establish the Vic Lewis Orchestra and to extend our musical horizons, this was also a time for much wild partying. The horrors of World War II behind us, we made up for lost time, letting the wine and the women take up their rightful places alongside the song.

Most of our hunting and wooing of fresh partners started around the Archer Street area of Soho, in the coffee bars and little clubs close to Mac's Rehearsal Room, the place where most of our working hours seemed to be spent when we were not on the road or in a studio. The legendary Windmill Theatre was just along the road.

The Windmill boasted, 'We never closed.' Unlike rival theatres all over London, the Windmill never did close throughout the war years. Servicemen around the world remember the Windmill for its immobile nude shows. The girls stood there on the stage statuelike, frozen in their semierotic poses for a series of tableaux which were claimed to be artistic and therefore acceptable under prevailing regulations for decency in the theatre. The rest of the Windmill's show consisted of variety turns between the tableaux. Many famous entertainers, including Bruce Forsyth and Harry Secombe, made some of their earliest appearances in these shows.

During rehearsal breaks we would surface from the 24-hour twilight of Mac's and take Windmill girls for a drink. Alternatively we'd leave little messages at their stage door, inviting favourite girls to join us before or after work.

At one point, I had been going out steadily for some time with a Windmill showgirl named Sylvia. Returning home to London after a gig in Blackpool, the band felt in precisely the right mood for the party we had arranged. I decided to check that everybody was coming by ringing round the likely girls. When I picked up the phone, I was surprised to hear Ken Thorne talking to my Sylvia from a bedroom extension upstairs.

I heard Sylvia saying to him, 'Have you told Vic you're taking me to the party? Does he know I'll be with you?' And when Ken did not reply immediately, she went on, 'Ken, you have told Vic about us, haven't you?' I was too flabbergasted to say a word. Then I heard Sylvia continue, 'Well, when you do tell him, make sure you remember to say I've fixed Moy to come over for him.' We did a fair bit of changing partners. Nothing was allowed to become too serious. If I fancied the girl Ronnie Chamberlain was seeing, I faced him with the problem and nobody would get upset. He would say, 'Vic, if you've fallen madly in love with my Beryl, feel free, my friend, have her for a fortnight.' What swines we were to all these gorgeous women!

There was one Windmill girl we would never dream of inviting to our outrageous parties. Jill Anstey was a person we wrote off as far too prim and proper for our style of affair, although one or two of us concealed an awful lust for her. Jill was a most beautiful girl, intelligent, around five foot four inches tall with long brown hair. Unlike the Bluebell Girls and other chorus girls, Windmill models did not have to be exceptionally tall. Her striking good looks and neatly proportioned figure attracted me at once. She did not drink, refused to sleep around with the boys and had a relatively quiet and reserved personality.

I had noticed Jill quite a few times with her friends in the Soho coffee bars. Our first real meeting came at a Sunday concert we did at the London Coliseum. Our singer at the time, Jacqueline Jennings, had also worked at the Windmill and several of her former colleagues came round backstage to see her at the end of the Coliseum show. One of these was Jill, who arrived in the dressing room on the arm of Bruce Forsyth. Bruce was very fond of jazz but, from what I gathered, an evening of our type of music was a rare experience for his date.

I fell head over heels in love with Jill at once. The stumbling block was that she had already involved herself pretty seriously with a very wealthy Indian and seemed to be on the verge of marrying him. This was in the spring of 1950, and I was about to go to New York. I pleaded with Jill to wait until I came back, to give our relationship a chance. I knew the offer of a much richer husband was weighing heavily on her mind and, when I left for New York, I was uncertain about the future of our romance.

•   •   •

At the end of 1949, I had enlarged the Vic Lewis Orchestra to a line-up that included five trumpets, five trombones and a four-man rhythm section. I wrote a piece called 'Music For Moderns' which we recorded in January 1950, using echo for the first time.

The way we achieved our echo effect was technologically primitive, but it worked. As a rule, the microphones set up in the studio would take the band's sound directly to the control room. We rerouted the lines to a basement toilet beneath the studios at EMI, Abbey Road. At one end of this small white-tiled room, we placed a loudspeaker. A couple of metres in front of it, we had a microphone to pick up the

**The Vic Lewis Music for Moderns
Orchestra with Jacqueline Jennings,
singer, at the Hammersmith Palais, 1950**

sound and take it back upstairs to the control room console. The gap between the speaker and the mike caused a slight delay and, combined with the natural echo in the toilet, resulted in the reverberation we were after.

'How did you get that fantastic sound on your new records?' Stan Kenton asked me when we met the same year. I thought the sound he was getting was great but Kenton insisted that our echo effect was better for this dramatic type of music.

Unfortunately, the huge sound of our enlarged line-up did not meet with enthusiasm in all quarters. A very small and discerning jazz public gave our first broadcast, on Monday 16 February, a favourable reception. Swiftly afterwards, I was summoned to the office of Jim Davison, programme head of BBC Light Music. He didn't pull his punch. 'If you play any more music like that, you'll be taken off the air.'

I kept my cool and began my reply unemotionally. 'I wouldn't want that to happen. However, if we don't go *on* the air, we can't be taken *off*. Let me put it another way; *stuff the BBC*!' This response kept me off the air for well over eight months.

Since 1948, I had been in regular contact with Stan Kenton, discussing, among other things, the ridiculous Musicians Union rule that had put a stop to all exchange of bands between Britain and America for well over twenty years. The source of the union deadlock had been a US radio broadcast made by Jack Hylton with his British musicians way back in 1926. Jack Hylton was one of Britain's most famous bandleaders. His publicity slogan was 'Jack's back' and posters all over London showed a pair of outstretched arms and a rear view of this rather short man. He toured the world in his heyday, before quitting to become an equally successful London impresario.

Militant American instrumentalists had attempted to outlaw Hylton's performance there, claiming that the bandleader should have recruited his men locally from US union membership. Hylton defied his angry opponents by doing his broadcast from a boat anchored beyond the maritime jurisdiction of American authorities. An exchange of retaliatory blows between British and American union bosses led to a stalemate. Working visits to either country by foreign jazz musicians were banned totally. London clubs lost their star attractions. American bands making European concert tours had to cross Britain off their itineraries. The only way an Englishman could work in an American band was by basing himself over there in alternative employment for at least a year.

Our Musicians Union in London saw itself as the great protector, preventing members from losing work to incoming foreigners. What really happened was that jazz in Britain stagnated. Unless musicians qualified as classical players, to whom the farcical rule did not apply, their only loophole was to come and go in the guise of variety acts, channelling their applications for work permits through the Variety Artists' Federation. British agents used the dodge to bring in a limited number of Americans; it seldom worked in reverse. This back-door operation further inflamed the MU, prolonging the bilateral ban on open exchanges.

Vic talks to Stan Kenton

Ever since my earliest trip to New York, I had recognised the damage being done to the cause of jazz in general by the continued imposition of the restrictions. My zealous interest in the music being played by America's progressive jazzmen led me to wage a personal war against the ban. I found a readily supportive ally in Stan Kenton and we agreed to tackle the unions together.

Kenton had expanded his band further than I had, and added sixteen strings, french horns and woodwind instruments. The normal jazz tempo had been four beats to a bar. Kenton and I decided to forget such boundaries and take any time signature we wanted. We would stop music in the middle, change the tempo, whatever. Influenced by modern classical music, we were ignoring traditional restrictions, and we were no longer performing music for dancing. The Vic Lewis

**Stan Kenton on stage at Carnegie Hall
in New York, 1950, flanked by his chief
arranger, Pete Rugolo, and Vic.
(Saxophones in the front row: Bob
Cooper, Art Pepper)**

Orchestra ceased to accept bookings to play in dance halls because people would
have found it impossible to do their traditional strict-tempo steps to our 'Music For
Moderns'.

Kenton was planning to present 'Innovations', his new music, at Carnegie Hall
in May 1950. He and I had held lengthy talks about the general concept and about
specific ideas and arrangements, and I was invited to conduct his large orchestra.

This provided the ideal opportunity for us to pursue the exchange agreement. I
obtained the blessing of the British MU, but not the authority to negotiate on their
behalf. I took Harold Davison with me to New York. In collaboration with Kenton
and his manager, we set up a meeting with the Musicians Union of America. It was
agreed that I should take back to the British MU for their approval the exchange
proposals Kenton and I had drafted. We would tour each other's country for three
weeks and the money I earned would be left in America for Stan Kenton while his
fees for performing in Britain would remain in London for me to pick up. In view of

Vic with June Christy, 1953

the fact that Kenton was famous in Britain and the Vic Lewis Orchestra was relatively unknown to Americans, Stan was clearly bending over backwards to cooperate.

Although the New York negotiations started promisingly, there was no positive outcome for a further six years. During that period, Harold Davison gradually replaced me as spokesman at union meetings in London, because too many of the dates clashed with my out-of-town band commitments.

In 1956, Stan Kenton brought his band to Britain and they became the first American musicians to play here in public for almost thirty years. That was the good news. The sad news was that Harold Davison's negotiating did not lead to the anticipated exchange deal for the Vic Lewis Orchestra after all. Instead, he booked Ted Heath's band to swop with Kenton. I felt terribly hurt that Harold should have done this to me.

Harold and I also went to see Frank Sinatra at New York's famous Copacabana. I asked him why he had not considered coming to Britain for concerts and Sinatra replied, 'I don't think there are any halls in England big enough for me.'

Before returning to London, I consolidated a number of friendships within the Kenton camp, particularly with June Christy, Shorty Rogers, Bud Shank, Maynard Ferguson, Bob Cooper, Milt Bernhart, Art Pepper and Shelly Manne, all of whom I made a point of staying in touch with during the years that followed.

June Christy was Kenton's singer. Shorty Rogers, one of Kenton's chief arrangers, still plays trumpet and flugelhorn. Bud Shank is recognised as one of the finest alto-sax players who ever lived; he doubles on flute. Maynard Ferguson's main claim to fame is that he hits notes higher than just about any other jazz trumpet player in the world. Bob Cooper, a tenor-sax player, was June's husband. Milt Bernhart played lead trombone. Art Pepper, the alto-sax player, and Shelly Manne, the drummer, two of the world's greatest, died in the early 1980s.

•   •   •

The moment our aircraft touched down in London, I telephoned Jill and was considerably relieved to learn that she had not made any irrevocable move in the direction of her Indian friend during my absence. I had to make for Sheffield to do a concert that same night but Jill joined me later and we spent a long romantic weekend getting to know one another a lot better. Soon after that, we went for a drive in Surrey one May afternoon and I proposed to her in the bar of a country pub. When she accepted, I bought her another large drink and gave her a nice ring.

By 1950 standards, it was a whirlwind courtship. We fixed the wedding for 28 July because my birthday is 29 July and I figured that I stood a fairer chance of remembering our anniversaries if the two dates were adjacent.

We had quite a simple little wedding at the Caxton Hall registry office with Harold Davison as my best man. Then we went back to his office in Shaftesbury Avenue where a few close friends sipped champagne and ate salt-beef sandwiches

Vic and Jill at Caxton Hall, 28 July 1950

with pickles, kindly supplied by the Nosh Bar, the nearby hang-out of both jazz musicians and Windmill girls. From there we hurried away to change at our new two-roomed home, a tiny flatlet at Endsleigh Court in Russell Square. We drove to Exeter, where we took a romantic evening stroll in the beautiful cathedral gardens before spending our first night together as a married couple. In the morning, we continued our journey down to Tintagel, in a most picturesque part of Devon.

When we walked into the restaurant of our hideaway honeymoon hotel at Tintagel for lunch, Jill and I were surprised to find ourselves the centre of attention, the other guests sniggering behind their menu cards or peeping out to stare at us. Then we opened the folded newspaper at our table and discovered that our wedding had made the front page. Fame at last!

Within a month of my marriage, I was forced to admit that the new 'Music For Moderns' orchestra faced financial failure. I had no personal or professional regret that I had put this big jazz band together. From an artistic viewpoint, the venture had been thoroughly rewarding, but there was no way we could continue to subsidise the swelling losses showing up on our balance sheets. The Beeb adamantly refused to give me any further bookings for a full eight months after the row that surrounded our debut broadcast with the big band back in February. Without proper radio exposure, we were denied not only the income but also the nationwide publicity that each BBC broadcast brought with it. The band could not exist even for another few months solely on concert appearances coupled with the slender hope of future record royalties.

With a heavy heart I took the decision to break up an aggregation that I still think of as one of the finest in the history of British big-band jazz. But I was determined to get back on my feet without delay.

I regrouped some of my finest musicians and formed a smaller, more viable band, borrowing the initial capital from my mother, who continued to have total faith in my musical integrity and was certain that our efforts would be successful in the end. As it happened, we were on the brink of far better fortune, for the middle fifties proved to be a marvellous time to lead a good band in Britain, the last golden era for our type of outfit.

By 1950, Ken Thorne had left us and returned to his mother in Cambridge. She never wanted him to play jazz in the first place. The truth is that all the way through the previous year I had watched Ken heading for a breakdown. He worked under constant pressure with the band, drinking a great deal too much, too early and for prolonged periods at a time. Added to this was the lingering legacy of childhood illness, which caused Ken to have a little less resilience than his relatively tough job with us demanded. I could see he was cracking up, although I was loath to lose either his companionship or his amazing musical abilities.

Ken's mother persuaded him to resume his church-organ studies at Ely Cathedral. She also put a block between the two of us for six or seven years after he went back to her. Occasionally, if I pestered him enough, he would send through an odd score, but we did not resume our close friendship until Ken was able to come to

London much later in a new role as the composer of film music. He went on to win an Oscar for orchestrating the film *A Funny Thing Happened on the Way to the Forum* and was responsible for the soundtrack scores of numerous other motion pictures, including the Beatles' *Help!*, the Monkees' *Head*, *The Bed-sitting Room* and *Murphy's War*, as well as the television series *The Persuaders*.

At first, during the latter half of 1950, I made mistakes over the type of work my latest band should take. We toured the major provincial theatres in the Moss Empires group, topping bills with variety stars like the comedian and singer Alfred Marks. We were on a percentage of the door. When we didn't draw in enough people, our own takings slumped but it was still down to us to settle the bills. By the autumn, a hasty rethink led us back in the direction of the ballrooms where we could balance our precise income more reliably against known expenses.

In 1951, we went on a tour of military bases and hospitals in Germany as part of a show built around Herb Jeffries, a great guy who had found fame with Duke Ellington in the forties. In America, Herb was a well-known singer, particularly remembered for his version of 'Flamingo'. On the last night of the tour, in Bad Nauheim, the entire cast of our show, including the comedy team of Morecambe and Wise and the ventriloquist Ray Allen, got together for farewell drinks.

Herb insisted that our bus driver should join the party, but the fellow wasn't too keen. 'This is OK for you lot but I need to be up at six in the morning. We have a 500-mile drive to the coast and you don't want to miss your ferry home, do you?'

Herb put a Scotch in the man's hand and an arm round his shoulder. 'Don't you worry about that, my friend. Just sit in this chair and face me. I am going to put you into a deep hypnotic trance. Every minute you are under the influence will be worth a full hour of normal sleep in your bed. Now, concentrate!'

Herb didn't wave a watch to and fro or get up to any of the conventional stage hypnotist's trickery. He placed a hand on our driver's forehead and the man appeared to go into a trance almost immediately. He gave all the outward signs of being fast asleep. Eric Morecambe was one of the more suspicious observers of this display. Herb was ready for him. 'I'll tell you what I'll do to convince you. I'm going to instil in this man's mind that he has forgotten to switch off his headlights and he'll race out to the bus as soon as he's awake.' Sure enough, that's exactly what our driver did.

Some of us still thought Herb had hired the driver as his stooge so Eric Morecambe agreed to be the subject of a further demonstration. When Eric was 'under', Herb told us, 'He's going to ask me for a cigarette when I bring him round – but he'll have to stub it out right away because the thing will taste like old rope. You can all offer him a smoke from your own packs but, until I give the word, they'll all taste ghastly.'

Eric reacted just as Herb had predicted, spluttering his way through initial puffs at half a dozen cigarettes, each one clearly causing him genuine discomfort. Eventually, Eric managed to have his first enjoyable smoke when Herb had given us a nod to expect that all would return to normal.

Herb Jeffries and Vic, 1951

Before Herb ended his impromptu act that night, it took a sinister turn for me. During this first year of our marriage, Jill had been travelling with me as much as possible when the band went on tour. She was always game for a laugh and needed no urging when I suggested that my last doubts about the true strength of Herb's strange hypnotic powers would vanish if she put herself forward as his final guinea pig of the evening.

Placing his hand on Jill's head, Herb put her 'under' and pulled off another humorous stunt of some sort. The amusing details of it were wiped from my memory by what happened a little later when Herb took me aside, warning me he had some bad news. By now he was speaking very gravely. 'Vic, I think your wife should see her doctor as soon as you get back to England. She's seriously unwell, you know.' Jill showed no signs of ill health and I was ready to write off Herb's chilling suggestion. The next night, less than twenty-four hours after the incident, Jill suddenly complained of abdominal pain so severe that I called in the doctor at once. He rushed her into hospital where she underwent urgent surgery for an ovarian cyst.

•   •   •

The Vic Lewis Orchestra at the Wood
Green Empire, late 1953: Brian
Rogerson, Bernard Allen, Ronnie
Chamberlain, Tubby Hayes, Les
Wingfield; Kenny Hollick on drums

By the end of the war, I had become an observer rather than a participant in cricket, merely reading the newspaper accounts of county cricket and touring team matches during the season. In 1951, when I was in Nottingham for several days with the band, I noticed that the South Africans were playing England at Trent Bridge. Jill was with me and I asked her casually how she felt about cricket. The game had faded so far towards the back of my mind that it was not a topic we had got around to discussing before. To my surprise, Jill told me she knew quite a few of the young Surrey players, Jim Laker and Alec and Eric Bedser for starters, and was very fond of the game.

I did not start playing again until I joined the Ravers, the side fielded by the staff of *Melody Maker*, the weekly music paper. In 1952, the band was playing in the ballroom of the County Hotel at Taunton in Somerset. My tour manager, Sid Maurice, approached the bandstand during our performance and said, 'Do you have any objection to a bunch of cricketers coming into the dance for the last hour?'

As a friend, Vic went along on Stan Kenton's 1953 tour of Europe and hung out with members of the band: June Christy, Frank Rossolino (trombone) and Zoot Sims (tenor sax), Conte Candoli (trumpet)

Of course I didn't. I suggested drinks afterwards. At one o'clock in the morning, Jill and I met George Dawkes, Les Jackson and most of the Derbyshire County cricket team in the lounge of our hotel. They were keen on talking about the band; I was much more interested in discussing their game. The outcome was that they enrolled me as a member of Derbyshire, promising to send me all the necessary papers, plus my tie, in the post. From this almost accidental incident stemmed my hobby of collecting cricket ties.

An array of colourfully striped club ties began to build up in our flat over the next few months. I was receiving more by each post. Eventually, Jill said, 'Vic, you really can't continue to accept all these ties without giving something back to people in return.' I saw the logic of this, so I formed the Vic Lewis Cricket Club and

Standing: Vic, Davy Schildkraute (alto sax), Zoot Sims, Stan Kenton, a french horn player, a Belgian club owner, Bill Holman (tenor sax and arranger); sitting: June Christy with Johnny Dankworth, who came over for the Brussels concert

designed a tie of my own. I decided on a three-colour design, purple, which was my own favourite colour, green, as in the grass of a cricket field, and blue, because blues is an essential component of jazz. The VLCC tie became much sought after. And everybody who became a patron of my club gave me a tie before he got one of mine.

• • •

In August 1952, the stresses of continual touring caught up with me. In one single day that month, the band was booked to play morning and afternoon sessions at Burtonwood American air base, and then a pair of evening concerts in Rochdale.

As usual in such situations, we drank an enormous amount of strong black coffee during breaks between performances. I noticed as the day wore on that I was developing a palpitation in the heart and, by the time our bus reached Rochdale, I was really worried. I changed to go on for the early evening show and convinced myself I didn't feel too bad.

About fifteen minutes into our performance, the palpitation turned into a pounding of the heart so forceful that I imagined I was on the point of death.

For the first and only time in my life, I lost my nerve completely in front of an audience. I rushed from the stage, asking my lead alto player, Ronnie Chamberlain, to take over and keep the show going. Our band manager, Sid Maurice, followed me out into the backstage car park and found me lurching around, clutching at my chest and breathing erratically.

The awful thumping inside my chest passed away almost as quickly as it had arrived. Had I been at home, I would have taken to my bed and called in the doctor. But we were due in Nottingham the next day and I pressed on.

During rehearsals at the Nottingham Astoria the following morning, I was conducting one of our new arrangements when I saw the music move off the staves. The hallucination grew worse, scaring the hell out of me. With intense horror, I watched a mass of distorted musical notes and lines entangle themselves until the whole page became a crazy and totally incomprehensible mess.

I dropped my bandleader's baton and fled blindly from the Astoria Ballroom, running, stumbling, running again, all the way back to our hotel. Jill had just arrived to join me for the weekend. I staggered into the room and collapsed at her feet. Bursting into uncontrollable tears, I bellowed hysterically, 'I can't go on, Jill! I'm finished!'

Jill took me back to London, a slow ten-hour drive, stopping at half-hour intervals while I vomited. When we arrived home, Jill summoned the doctor. He examined me and advised me to give up touring completely.

The age of the pop idols

Frankie Laine, Johnnie Ray, Bill Haley

EIGHT WEEKS AFTER the incidents in Rochdale and Nottingham in 1952, I felt I had to return to the band. Although I looked forward to a reunion with the boys, I was deeply concerned about my ability to cope with taking up a bandleader's baton again and appearing before the public. I met up with the band at Hinckley, in Leicestershire, and everyone welcomed me back, made a big fuss and did all they could to put me at ease. As I stood behind the drapes at the side of the stage that night, waiting for my cue to walk out there, nightmarish memories of racing off during the show at Rochdale flashed before my eyes. I turned to Sid Maurice and said quietly, 'I'm going to need a very large whisky before I can go on.'

From that time until the end of my bandleading days in 1960, I never ventured onto a stage without swallowing at least one large Scotch. In the interval, I became accustomed to topping up with one or two more doubles. And I made sure there was a new bottle ready to open in the dressing room at the end of the show. On reflection, I must admit that this was a silly way of dealing with my problems. What started as a swift stimulant at the opening of each performance developed into nothing less than a potentially dangerous addiction to alcohol. Drinking in that way is neither healthy nor particularly enjoyable.

One day in 1953, Harold Davison rang to say he had fixed an engagement for the band at the Colston Hall in Bristol, where we would be accompanying an American singer named Frankie Laine, who was at number one in the charts with 'I Believe'. Laine had more than half a dozen million-selling records to his credit, including 'Jezebel' and 'Mule Train'. The critics called him 'the man with the leather lungs'. He went on to push more than a score of best-selling singles into the hit parade over a ten-year period. In 1953 Laine was approaching the peak of his popularity with British pop fans.

To a jazzman, the stuff Frankie Laine was selling so lucratively seemed banal and, since Laine had his own conductor, I didn't even stay in the theatre to watch his act. I was amazed when Harold called me the next day to say that Frankie Laine

Jill with Frankie Lane and Al Lerner (right) at Stoke-on-Trent, 1953

Vic with Johnnie Ray at the Royal Command Performance, London, 1955

was insisting we should be with him for every single date he did over here in the future. And soon Frank and I became the firmest of friends.

The next pop star to call for our band's accompaniment in concert was Laine's stablemate at Columbia Records in America, the 'Cry Guy' himself, Johnnie Ray. In the early fifties, Ray had million-sellers in the emotion-charged ballads 'Cry' and 'Little White Cloud That Cried', during which the singer actually burst into tears. Ray was accompanied by my musicians on a tour which included Britain, Ireland and France, and at the 1955 Royal Variety Performance in front of the Queen – a proud highlight of my band's career.

Wherever he went, he was mobbed by fans. In South Africa, the reception for Johnnie Ray was most sensational of all. After tremendous scenes in Johannesburg and Cape Town, Johnnie flew into Durban, where the airport was about six miles from the city centre. A convoy of open limousines was waiting to take us to our hotel and I sat in the first one, beside John. All the way into town, the route was lined with wildly cheering fans; I was told this was the most amazing welcome Durban had ever given to any visiting star. At the hotel, I jumped clear of our limo just as John submerged beneath a seething mass of fanatical teenagers.

I raced indoors and attempted to rally additional police support. We fought our way back to the roadside, where I could see that Ray was bleeding from the forehead and his hearing aid had been pulled out. By now, I was seriously concerned for our star's safety. With his feet scarcely touching the ground, he was handed over the heads of the crowd in a prone position until he crash-landed unceremoniously at our feet inside the hotel entrance. I was furious that the security forces had not prevented this, and expected John to be equally angry. Far from it!

Picking himself up off the floor, he plugged the hearing aid back into his ear and turned to me, grinning broadly. 'Gosh, Vic, that was some fun! They seem to love me here.' And he winked as he began signing autographs for a bunch of young hotel guests.

Something that did make Johnnie Ray justifiably angry in South Africa was the barring of blacks from the theatres where he was appearing. One day when he had some free time, he hired a truck, loaded a piano on the back and did his show in a black township. The impromptu performance went down a storm.

At a reception held in Johannesburg City Hall, I was seated next to a prominent government minister. I took the opportunity of raising very gently the question of apartheid segregating concert audiences. He told me unemotionally that there was no reason why we could not play to a black audience, if we could find a theatre. Of course, that was the catch. It proved quite impossible to find a place to put on a show.

While in South Africa, I was much influenced by the tribal singing I heard in the townships, together with the curiously hypnotic sounds created with the use of penny whistles and drums by untrained but musical black instrumentalists. I wrote a suite lasting almost an hour, featuring items entitled 'Natal', 'Gold Dust', 'The Jacaranda Tree', 'Eastern And Western Province', 'Orange Free State' and 'The

Vic meets an ethnic influence in Durban

Jill and Vic with Guy Mitchell, 1955, backstage at the London Palladium

Voortrekkers' March'. Several of these pieces were recorded and others I was able to use in broadcasts.

Our tours of various territories with Johnnie Ray convinced me that musical entertainment in general was entering a fresh phase, when the pop idol would dominate the international show-business scene. This phase lasted until the early sixties, when the Beatles brought beat groups into fashion and solo singers were put out in the cold again. Meanwhile, since every singing star needed support from a band of backing musicians, the future for the Vic Lewis Orchestra in the middle fifties looked reasonably good.

After Frankie Laine and Johnnie Ray, other singers, including Billy Daniels, Mel Torme, the Hi-Los, Martha Ray and Guy Mitchell, walked out in front of my band to perform for their European fans. Many great singers and musicians worked for me during this period. On saxophone I had, at various times, Ronnie Chamberlain, Kathleen Stobart, Tubby Hayes, Ronnie Scott, Derek Humble, Vic Ash and Bob Efford. On trumpet I used Kenny Wheeler, Ron Simmonds, Stan Reynolds, Hank Shaw and Jimmy Ducher. Among the singers with the band were Denny Dennis, Terry Devon, Edna Kaye and Pearl Carr. Our arranging staff, after Ken Thorne, included John Keating, Edwin Holland, Bill Oliver and an American contingent led by Gerry Mulligan, Bill Holman, Shorty Rogers and Bill Russo.

Running a big band in the fifties involved the periodic swallowing of one's pride. I stuck my neck out to play the kind of music I loved, but I was obliged to compromise from time to time or we would never have survived. On one occasion, in Sunderland, as I helped to unpack our instruments, a man came up and plonked down a large metronome in front of our music stands at the centre of the stage. 'Tonight, as you must know, Mr Lewis, we're holding our Strict Tempo Ballroom Dancing Championships. This metronome will assist you to regulate your tempo accurately for the slow foxtrot, the waltz, the quickstep, et cetera.'

I bent down, picked up the metronome and gave him the polite version of what I thought he should do with the pointed end. 'My band plays the beat I give them.'

Afterwards, a number of the dancers congratulated the band on the evening's music. The winning couple said, 'If the dancers are up to scratch, they'll fit in their steps to the tempo being played.'

I hate ballroom dancing. After playing for dancers, on and off, over a period of twenty years, I was still unable to do a single step myself.

• • •

I learned to play trombone at High Wycombe during the war when Don Macaffer, the trombonist with the Buddy Featherstonhaugh Sextet, helped me to understand the workings of his instrument. Eventually I bought my own. I found I needed to express my musical personality in more forceful and direct terms than the guitar permitted. The tune part of a jazz piece could be performed much more effectively on something like the trombone. But I was never good enough to join the trombone section of any band full time. I don't think my lip was strong enough. I used to blow so loud I made blood come out into the mouthpiece.

**Vic meets Lena Horne at the London
Casino in the early 1950s**

In the Jazzmen after the war, the guitar became a key element of our sound and I concentrated on that instrument for the rest of my bandleading career. It would in any case have been difficult to conduct, do the occasional vocal and be a trombonist at the same time. I made a few recordings as a trombone player and, on the strength of these, people voted for me in the music-paper popularity polls, putting me high up on the list of favourite solo trombone jazzmen.

I kept my trombone to play occasionally for pleasure, I played it once with Kenton when one of his regular musicians in that section was ill, and later I had the opportunity to play it with Louis Armstrong.

When I first saw Armstrong, as a teenage lad in the early thirties, at the Ambassador cinema in Hendon, I made myself known to the great man, saying I was an up-and-coming guitarist with professional ambitions and would like to run a Louis Armstrong appreciation society in Britain. It was a rare treat for me and the band when we were asked to support him on his UK concert tour in the spring of 1956.

The highlight of each evening for me came during the finale of the show when I joined the Armstrong aggregation on stage to play my trombone alongside that of Trummy Young. With Ed Hall on clarinet, Billy Kyle on piano, Barrett Deems on drums and Jack Lesburg on bass, we riffed and played 'When The Saints Go Marching In'.

During that tour, I spent a series of wonderful nights in the company of Armstrong and Doc Schiff. Schiff was a staunch pal of Armstrong, an aide who helped him to feel secure just by being around him constantly. I have no idea whether he possessed any formal medical qualifications but he was 'Doc' to Louis and the rest of us. His main function appeared to be to make sure Armstrong's bowels worked. We shared hilarious conversations on the nature and frequency of the jazzman's motions. The pair of them advocated the absolute importance of a good purgative. To ensure regularity, Louis carried great cartons of an American brand of laxative with him wherever he travelled, explaining that life would not be worthwhile without his daily dose.

●   ●   ●

Vic on stage at Earl's Court with Louis Armstrong, 1956

Vic on trombone, deputising for Bob Fitzpatrick who was taken short before a Stan Kenton concert at the Alhambra, Paris, 1956

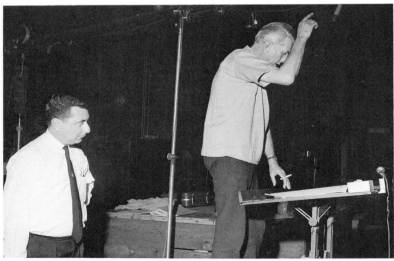

Vic watches Stan Kenton recording *West Side Story* at Samuel Goldwyn Studios in Hollywood, 1960

On 19 April 1956 Prince Rainier of Monaco married the screen star Grace Kelly. Stan Kenton, who was working in Europe at this time, was invited to write a ballet for the wedding celebrations. He had to tell Monaco's consul in London that it would be impossible to create something completely new for this occasion. Stan explained his dilemma to me, saying, 'Vic, the prince's people are still keen to have one of my works for this royal ballet. Do you think we can do something together?'

Kenton came to our tiny two-roomed flat in Russell Square, WC1, accompanied by the distinguished choreographer Anton Dolin, and, while Jill plied us with an endless supply of hot coffee and sandwiches, we worked through the night to make a complete ballet from existing scores. We played appropriate parts of various Kenton recordings to Anton, who promised he could put the choreography together if we did the music. We called the arranger Johnny Richards in New York for help, giving him the bar numbers over the transatlantic line.

The finished work, 'Homage To A Princess', was performed on the night of the wedding in Monte Carlo.

When the London Festival Ballet decided to put this in their performance, I was invited by the conductor, Norman Del Mar, to go down and run through parts of the orchestrations, particularly explaining the Kentonian playing of backbeats, not a normal element of classical music.

•　　•　　•

After the thirty-year ban on exchange trips by American and British jazzmen was finally lifted in 1956, the Vic Lewis Orchestra toured America four times. I marked the first occasion by writing a suite, using titles of personal significance: 'The Forrest' (because the band stayed at the hotel of that name in New York city), 'Dobbs Ferry' (the home town of the bandleader and arranger Johnny Richards, with whom Stan Kenton and I had so recently worked on the Monaco ballet), and 'Beau Kai' (my version of a trombone solo I had written for a great friend from Denmark, Kai Winding). Another tune from this suite, which we also recorded, was 'Pennsylvania Turnpike'.

On our first tour we were part of an enormous stage package billed as 'the Greatest Show of 1956'. The headlining act was Bill Haley and his Comets. The rest of the show was dominated by black rock-and-rollers ranging from Clyde McPhatter to Chuck Berry, from the Teenagers featuring Frankie Lymon to the Platters. Also on the bill were the Flares, a vocal group, and a big band fronted by Buddy Johnson. After our opening night, at Providence, Rhode Island, Bud Johnson took me aside to give me a large whisky and some good advice.

Our band's spot had gone down badly with a crowd of hostile American teenagers. Bud said, 'Hey, man, you've just got to learn the rock beat.' In musical terms, it was a matter of emphasising the second and fourth beat in each bar. To my ears, this made everything sound the same. Bud gave us a number from his library, 'Doot Doot Dow', and took us through some remarkable choreographical move-

The Vic Lewis Orchestra stop near Newport, Connecticut, on their last US tour, 1960: Ray Dempsey (guitar), Terry Shannon (piano), Shirley Gray (vocal), Roy East (alto sax), Arthur Watts (bass), Gordon Turnbull (trumpet), Jimmy Ducher (trumpet), Keith Christy (trombone), Vic Ash (tenor sax and clarinet), Art Elefson (tenor sax), Allan Ganley (drums), Ronnie Ross (baritone sax), Leon Calvert (trumpet)

The Vic Lewis Orchestra in 1959 with Dudley Moore (front, left) and singer Irma Logan, in the snow near Boston

The Platters with Vic at York, 1958

Bill Haley and his Comets arrive in Dublin, 1958

ments which would have driven 'em wild back home in the palm courts of Bournemouth. All this was absolutely alien to us and against our musical beliefs, and I felt my musicians deserved better.

Throughout that long, hot, late-summer month, in venues all across the United States, I watched excited and overheated teenagers turn on to a new breed of pop idol. They roared and yelled for Bill Haley's mob and the later legendary rhythm-and-blues giants on our tour bill. What chance had sixteen white bandsmen from Britain now that rock and roll had burst upon the scene? No sooner had the ban on visiting foreign musicians finished than we faced this fresh threat.

On our second tour of America, in 1958, most of the dates were university campus concerts, where we encountered some of our most satisfying and satisfied US audiences. In 1959, most of the dates on our third tour took us to military establishments all over America.

Dudley Moore joined the band to play piano with us in 1959. He came straight from Oxford, and it took him some time to stop calling me 'sir'. During this US tour together, Dudley and I became very good friends. When I formed my agency, less than a couple of years later, he was my first client. That relationship did not last long, simply because Dudley decided to become involved with a show called *Beyond the Fringe* instead of continuing to concentrate his career on playing jazz.

The band's fourth and final tour of America was early in 1960. We were billeted at a naval base outside New York. For the duration of our stay, we were given officer rank. Our last engagement on that tour was a dream come true. We played at Birdland on Broadway, New York's mecca of fine jazz, with the Lee Konitz Quartet as our relief group. Every man in the band was nervous, but I think the tension helped us to turn in a good performance. The rest of the help came from the jazz greats who were in the audience to support us. The star-stacked guest list included Sarah Vaughan and Carmen McRae, who rate second only to Ella Fitzgerald as jazz singers, Maynard Ferguson, Zoot Sims, Buddy Rich and a host of others. This was our farewell appearance in front of an American audience. It was a splendid way for the band to bow out.

The kids of Britain soon discovered rock and roll through imported records and the soundtracks of films such as *Blackboard Jungle* and *Rock Around the Clock*. Although I continued to lead the Vic Lewis Orchestra until after our last US tour, these were not our happiest times. The final years were a curious mixture of spasmodic success and insidious decline, musical compromise and dwindling funds. We still toured the UK with various visiting acts, particularly the Platters and Bill Haley and his Comets. The Comets were a bunch of great guys but Haley himself, poor chap, believed his own fantastic publicity.

In my opinion, Bill Haley wasn't even a mediocre musician. He was a showman, and it was gimmickry rather than deep-rooted creative talent that took him to the top. Cut off that kiss curl coming down over the centre of Haley's forehead, forget all the eccentric choreography of having mature men lying supine on the floor to play their instruments, and Haley had little to offer.

Second Innings

Jill and Danielle, 1983

From Birdland
to the Blue Lagoon

Danielle and William Victor Productions

HAD IT NOT been for the stalwart financial support I received from my mother, the band would have faced collapse earlier. My weekly outgoings in the form of retainers to my musicians exceeded £1000, which had to be paid out whether the work came in or not. Soon after the last US tour I took the problem to my manager, Harold Davison, and told him that I was heavily in debt not only to the bank but to my mother. In the absence of fresh bookings for the band, he had to agree that we had no alternative but to call it a day and break up the Vic Lewis Orchestra.

The time had also come for me to remind Harold of our earliest deal. 'We did agree at the beginning that I would come in with you as a partner in our own agency business when the bandleading days were over. How do we stand now, Harold?'

He looked straight back at me and replied unemotionally, 'Ah, Vic, the business has changed a lot since then.' He offered me £20 a week.

'And what sort of split are we talking about on commission monies?'

'We're not talking commissions here, Vic.'

'I already give my mother £20 a week, Harold.'

I had to make the best of Davison's unattractive offer without further argument, because Jill had become pregnant at last. It had taken us ten long years, but Jill finally presented me with our only child, a daughter we named Danielle, on 11 June 1960.

If Danielle had been a boy, I am certain she would have made a great cricket player. From the time she was three weeks old, she came to matches with me every Sunday. Despite all this conditioning, Danielle took up tennis. She qualified through the Lawn Tennis Association and the American coach system and is now a professional tennis coach and the LTA's London development officer.

When Danielle was born, we moved from our small Russell Square flat, a place which had a wealth of personal and musical memories for me. Endsleigh Court must have been one of the most swinging apartment blocks in central London during the fifties. Our neighbours included Ronnie and Mabel Chamberlain, Jack

Parnell and Tito Burns. Ronnie had worked with me since the days of the Jazzmen. He was my lead alto man and a wonderful soprano and clarinet player. After twelve years, Ronnie allowed himself to be lured away from our orchestra by Ted Heath.

Jill and I made our new home in Marlow Court, Willesden Lane, where there was more room to raise Danielle. When our daughter was about eighteen months old, I returned home from work one evening to find Willesden Lane blocked off by police cars and a convoy of fire engines parked outside our block of flats. A constable held me back, flagging down the car. 'No further, sir. There's been a serious accident here.' In my panic to find out what had become of Jill and the baby, I abandoned my car at the kerbside and ran blindly towards our building.

I was confronted with a strange sight. A twin-seater aircraft had crashed through the roof. Fuel from its damaged tanks was leaking dangerously to the floors below. A number of housewives had fled from their kitchens, leaving gas cookers alight, and the fire brigade feared the whole place might explode at any minute. The good news was that I found Jill and Danielle, both unharmed and quite safe. The bad news was that Jill had been pregnant with our second child and this upset caused her to have a miscarriage.

• • •

Within a week of sitting down at my new desk in Harold Davison's offices, I sold the Count Basie orchestra for a date in Plymouth at £2000, twice the fee other bookers were getting. This convinced me that, given decent financial backing, I could set up my own agency. After all, I knew a whole range of artists, managers and bookers throughout the world.

In search of capital, I turned to an eighteen-stone giant of a man, Bill Benny, who wrestled professionally as 'Man Mountain Benny' and owned a couple of social clubs in Manchester. Bill had been a big fan of my music from the time I formed the big band. He had even travelled all the way over to New York to attend our farewell bash at Birdland, bringing with him one of his best friends, a rising disc jockey named Jimmy Savile. Bill became my partner and put up £20,000. Our business title became William Victor Productions, derived from our two first names. In September 1960, I found a convenient little office at 190 Piccadilly and hired a secretary. The fact that we were operating from a single room was offset by the prestigious address. We divided the organisation into two. A production company, which promoted shows and concert tours, and the Vic Lewis Agency.

Soon after signing Dudley Moore as my first agency client, I added the West Indian bandleader Leslie 'Jiver' Hutchinson to our initial roster. Jiver was one of the few surviving members of the ill-fated Ken 'Snakehips' Johnson Band, most of whose musicians had been killed instantly when the Kit Kat Club was bombed during a wartime air raid on London. I had known Jiver since the war days but it was his daughter who became the agency's first new star, under the name of Elaine Delmar.

To Vic
With Best Wishes
From 'Your Star'
Elaine

Elaine Delmar, 1960. Her big chance came as an understudy in the West End production of the Richard Rodgers musical *No Strings*, when she replaced the star at the dress rehearsal

The first engagement I booked for the Hutchinson band with Elaine as their singer was at a place in the Cambridge area. It turned out to be a debut date with a tragic twist. In the middle of the night, I took a telephone call from a tearful Elaine, telling me the band's bus had crashed. 'My father is dead, Vic. Jiver has been killed.' The poor girl recovered bravely from that traumatic experience, and developed into the truly great jazz singer I always knew she deserved to become.

In the initial stages, I had to go to Harold Davison for many of the international entertainers he was bringing into Britain at the time. It meant paying Davison's inflated prices, but it helped to establish the image and good reputation of William Victor Productions when we were able to put our name above the billing for a wealth of successful presentations.

When Judy Garland was to appear for us in Manchester, Harold asked me to take the entourage by train from London. Her party included her teenage daughter, Liza. Although Judy's concert performances had passed their artistic peak, she still generated her own special electricity throughout the auditorium from the moment she walked out on a stage.

Judy Garland's favourite drink was chilled Liebfraumilch. The moment she had settled into her Manchester hotel suite, she asked me to get her some. 'I'll need some when I get there, a little more to sip between the shows, and, of course, plenty to offer people afterwards. In fact, I'll want my wine most of the time I'm not on stage.'

I much enjoyed the many bottles of the stuff she shared with me that night in Manchester. I found the lady quite charming, although somewhat eccentric.

I saw Judy Garland two or three times in New York after that. She always greeted me with 'Hi, Vic, baby!' The final time I saw Judy was frightening. I was flying from Los Angeles to New York, en route for home. As I boarded the aircraft, I noticed in the first seat on my right this little old lady, weighing, I imagine, no more than 80 or 90 pounds. 'Hi, Vic, baby!' she whispered weakly. My final glimpse of her was in the baggage-claim hall after the flight. She was with some young chap and this really did tug at my heartstrings.

While I was in Los Angeles on a later trip, I saw Liza Minnelli give her first solo performance. I was completely captivated with her, recognising so many of the mother's finest talents in the daughter.

Harold Davison asked me to do him a favour by looking after Paul Robeson when the singer came to London on his way back to the States from Russia. Harold had rented Robeson a flat in town and for a fortnight I kept him and his wife company. He was an ailing man but we established a good rapport in a short time. He wanted some rare 12-inch 78-r.p.m. HMV Red Label records of a great Russian bass singer, and after trudging round all the specialist shops in central London, I came across a complete set of these deleted discs at the Gramophone Exchange in Wardour Street. Paul Robeson's face lit up when he saw the goodies I had brought him. His delight made the day-long search worthwhile.

Another artist Harold asked me to look after around this time, in 1960, was

Carmen McRae in London, 1960

Carmen McRae, who became a close family friend. Carmen wanted some jewellery while she was in London. Through old trade contacts of my father's, I managed to do a remarkably good deal for her, and she was impressed. She and I made many happy shopping expeditions around the West End.

Bill Benny's club interests in Manchester represented the humble beginnings of an enormous cabaret boom that swept the north of England in the early sixties and later the whole country. This type of venue, offering late-night live entertainment, replaced the old variety theatres for many people. These clubs usually had a restaurant and casino. Bill was boss of the Cabaret and the Devonshire in Manchester and several suburban places in the vicinity. At the Free Trade Hall in Manchester, Bill and I presented the singers Ella Fitzgerald, Sarah Vaughan, Nat King Cole and Shirley Bassey, the pianist George Shearing, and the comedian Bob Hope. After their concerts, most of our bill-toppers came down to Bill's Cabaret Club for dinner, an added thrill for his clientele. Our largest stars used to receive between 80 and 90 per cent of the takings at the door, or up to £3000, for a pair of Free Trade Hall performances.

Soon it seemed ridiculous to continue handing part of the proceeds to Harold Davison. I felt I owed the fellow few favours. One day I told Bill Benny, 'I'm going to America. I must start signing up my own acts.'

Ella Fitzgerald and Vic with Shelly Manne, mid-1960s

Ella Fitzgerald outside the Hammersmith Odeon, 1960

Sarah Vaughan and Vic, 1961

**Nelson Riddle and Vic visit Frank
Sinatra in a London recording studio,
June 1962**

My first stateside trip as a seeker of talent was successful, and I managed to take
in some jazz on the side. In 1961, I took Bill Benny with me on my next US visit.
During our stay I met Nelson Riddle, a conductor and arranger who became a close
friend until his death in 1985. Riddle was achieving considerable fame for his
recordings with Frank Sinatra and Nat King Cole. He had started to make his own
orchestral albums and was gaining a reputation for the scores he turned out for
motion pictures. I suggested he might tour the UK and we went ahead with putting
together a package consisting of Shirley Bassey, the Hi-Los vocal group and Nelson
Riddle's orchestra. While Riddle was in London, I arranged for him to record two
albums, one with Bassey and one with Danny Williams, a young South African who
sang in the style of Johnny Mathis. Shirley's included one of my original tunes
called 'I Can't Get You Out Of My Mind', and Danny recorded another original of
mine, which Nelson scored, entitled 'Once Upon A Time'.

The Hi-Los on the Scottish border

Nelson Riddle on the beach at Malibu

Shirley Bassey in Sydney Botanical Gardens, 1963

When Nelson came to Britain, I took him and one of his sons, Christopher, to Lord's cricket ground. While I left them briefly to go for a tinkle, a local youngster walked up to Nelson and said, 'Excuse me, but was that really the famous Vic Lewis you were with just before?'

Through my partnership with Bill Benny and our concert promotion activities in Manchester, I became, for a time, personal manager to Shirley Bassey. On her best nights, she was an exceptional performer, but her temperament left a lot to be desired.

At the end of the 1950s a small London club, the Blue Lagoon in Carnaby Street, instigated a brave new policy of presenting major jazz singers on a regular basis. The owner, Bill Manning, approached me for American attractions. I brought Bill Manning many of the world's greatest female singers. My list included Helen Merrill, Monica Zetterlund, Ethel Ennis, Abbey Lincoln, Teri Thornton, Elaine Delmar, Donna Hightower and – the greatest of them all in my opinion –

Fresh from holiday in the West Indies, Vic helps Frankie Vaughan clear the streets of New York, 1959

**Vic, Elvis Presley, Bill Benny and
Colonel Tom Parker in Hollywood, 1961**

Dinah Washington. If she had lived, I'm sure Dinah would have graduated into the same league as Fitzgerald and Vaughan.

The Blue Lagoon had a friendly atmosphere and became a favourite meeting place for the cricket fraternity. I have always found there to be a fair proportion of jazz devotees among cricket players. One Saturday night in the summer of 1959, I had arranged to meet Gary Sobers, Collie Smith and Tom Dewdney, a trio of terrific West Indian test players, at the Blue Lagoon. They were due to drive down from the north in readiness to play a charity match in the Vic Lewis Cricket Club team in London on the Sunday. At ten o'clock that evening I received a telephone call telling me the party's car had crashed at Stoke and the three boys had been rushed off to hospital. Poor Collie died and the Blue Lagoon never had the same appeal for me afterwards.

• • •

Bill Benny was an ardent fan of Elvis Presley. In 1961 I set up a meeting for us in Hollywood with Presley's manager, Colonel Tom Parker, and then broke the news to my partner. 'Bill, we're lunching today with Colonel Parker and Elvis Presley.' His eyes widened and a huge smile spread across his face. We drove to the Samuel Goldwyn film studios and went through the whole security rigmarole of presenting identification and obtaining visitors' passes.

We were ushered into a huge and lavishly furnished office where most of one vast wall was covered by a larger-than-life-size portrait – not of Presley but of Parker. Then the great man himself joined us. Not Presley but Parker.

'Welcome, gentlemen!' roared Parker, pumping our hands with vigour. 'My boy is still on the film set but they'll stop shooting for the lunch break any moment and I'll bring him right down to meet you all.'

Elvis Presley turned up, attired in yachting gear. He struck me as being shy, unsure of himself in the company of businessmen and surprisingly unsophisticated for a star of his stature.

We enjoyed an excellent lunch and Elvis gave each of us a copy of his *Blue Hawaii* album. After the meal, Elvis returned to face the cameras for an afternoon's work while we got down to serious discussion with Parker about the possibility of a European concert tour. Colonel Parker's terms were quite concise. 'If we come to England, gentlemen, I want all the cash to go to charity. I want to play at Wembley Stadium and I want the owners to make no rental charges for our use of the venue. All the refreshments are to be given away free to the fans – the Coke, the ice cream, that stuff.' The Colonel paused only briefly to draw breath. 'I want the use of our own chartered Boeing jet to fly the entourage from Los Angeles to London and back. Finally, I would need your personal guarantee that the Queen of England would be our guest of honour. A royal charity gala at Wembley Stadium! That's the way I want to do it!'

We said our formal farewells to Parker, wishing his client all possible success. I promised the Colonel I would see what we could do about his concert proposals, but Bill and I knew we had no chance of satisfying his conditions.

Glamour,
glitter and dirty tricks

Johnny Mathis, Donovan, Andy Williams

INEVITABLY, DURING THE earliest days of William Victor Productions, the agency took second place to our concert-promotion activities, although I dabbled in the representation of a few pop singers. In 1961 our reputation as agents and our roster of acts grew.

We expanded our headquarters from one room to three but stayed in the same building in Piccadilly. I took on an assistant, Don Black, who proved to be a good booker and a man who enjoyed hard work. He had been a reporter with the pop paper *New Musical Express*, and was now managing one of Britain's best-known ballad singers of the era, Matt Monro. This smooth-voiced former bus conductor notched up almost a dozen singles in the charts during the first half of the sixties. With Don's painstaking help, Matt Monro moved on to become a concert and cabaret star.

Don Black's main love in life was lyric writing. He showed every sign of emerging as an exceptionally able songwriter and turned out a lot of first-class material for Matt. Shortly after he joined the Vic Lewis Agency, he collaborated with me on a number of songs. The partnership worked admirably. I had been in negotiation with Oriole Records and was on the verge of doing a deal which would let me arrange and sometimes conduct my own songs for acts I represented. I had also discussed a deal with the music publisher Dick James. I could not resist giving the new companies which grew from these arrangements a cricketing connection. We named our recording firm Oval Productions and the songwriting company was called Lords.

Before long, artists and their managers were coming to us for original compositions. In 1964, for instance, the manager of the Irish group the Bachelors asked us for a new number for the group's recording session the following day. The Bachelors had enjoyed success with 'Ramona' and 'Diane' that year and were searching for something in similar vein, and suitable for the American market. In eight minutes flat, Don and I concocted a song entitled 'Maureen' which the three

Bachelors recorded the next day for American release. It gave them a moderately big hit in that territory.

Our next joint venture as writers involved a singer I had seen in a Broadway musical. Having watched her show six times, I had fallen hopelessly in love with Diahann Carroll. I made contact and discovered that she was scheduled to visit London, and promised her that Don and I would have four new songs ready by the time she arrived. I still think that two of those four, 'Have I Changed?' and 'My Room', represent the finest work Don and I ever did together. When I brought the fabulous New York singer, Teri Thornton, to London we wrote another four custom-tailored songs and recorded them with the unusual backing of five flutes and five french horns. These were scored by Johnny Keating, who had been an arranger and lead trombone player with my 1950 band. (He had left me to join Ted Heath's band and became Heath's chief arranger before going to Hollywood to write film scores.) But none of these songs had the success they deserved.

A third lady for whom Don and I put together four original songs was a close friend of mine from Kenton days, June Christy. She had a husky, smoky voice that set her apart from most jazz vocalists. I assembled a little group, featuring Tubby Hayes on tenor saxophone. Victor Feldman arranged and conducted. One of the items we recorded with June was called 'The Cool Elephant', named after a London night spot for which I was booking the cabaret acts and where I had arranged a residency for Dudley Moore's trio.

The biggest hit that Don and I wrote together was 'My Child', originally earmarked for Barbra Streisand until her manager demanded publishing rights – we had already placed the song with our own music-publishing company, Lords. Keely Smith, a jazz singer with a drawling Southern accent, got as far as taping 'My Child', but her version was never issued because we refused for a second time to hand over publishing rights as part of the recording deal. It was third time lucky when the popular Connie Francis released 'My Child' in 1965 and it became a bestseller. Apart from 'My Child', one of our most successful compositions was 'Beyond The Hill', a worldwide hit for Matt Monro, for whom we also wrote 'When You Become A Man'. Wendy Craig used the latter title as the theme for her television series at the time.

I was sad when the writing partnership of Don Black and Vic Lewis petered out after producing something like forty compositions. Don Black went on to collaborate with an assortment of talented partners, including Elmer Bernstein, Henry Mancini, Michel Legrand and Andrew Lloyd Webber. I was reunited with Don Black in 1981 when we wrote 'Diana' together to mark the wedding of Prince Charles and Lady Diana, and it was recorded by Matt Monro. After my short partnership with Don, I wrote many orchestra pieces as well as vocal compositions, and conducted a number of instrumental recordings in a variety of musical settings. I was particularly proud of one piece, 'The Other Woman', which featured the great trumpet player Maynard Ferguson. This was one of the tracks that made up the second side of my *Russian Suite* album.

Don Black, Diahann Carroll and Vic, 1965

June Christy and Vic in Balboa, California, 1960

One of the first people ever to collaborate with me on a song was Johnnie Ray. He had happened to hear me playing a particular piece at many different parties. Intrigued by the tune, he came up with a set of really lovely lyrics and we recorded the song together under the title 'My Love For You'. Other people who occasionally collaborated with me as lyricists were the singer Julie London's husband Bobby Troup (who wrote 'Route 66'), Robin Gibb of the pop group the Bee Gees, and Randy Edelman, an inventive American lyricist, composer, pianist and vocalist who has recorded a number of albums and singles and written hit songs for other artists, including Barry Manilow. Randy and his wife, Jackie DeShannon, and their son Noah have become close friends of the family.

Throughout my recording career, as a bandleader or arranger or songwriter, I picked up knowledge of record production by observing what was happening up in the control room. After conducting a piece, I would go into the 'box' and discuss the recording with the producer. By the time I decided to produce in my own right, I had a stockpile of knowledge to call on, having been involved in recording-studio techniques from other viewpoints. Great expertise in a technical or technological field has never been essential because the studio engineer at the session takes care of all the mechanics of controlling the knobs and switches. The engineer acts on his producer's instructions. If asked to make an oboe louder, for example, it is up to the engineer to shift a microphone closer to the musician or to increase the volume via the appropriate knob on his control console.

I did a great deal of recording for Oval Productions; the resulting material was issued in the early stages on NEMS Records and later on the CBS label, which distributed NEMS. Using the virtuoso talents of the classical guitarist John Williams, with a full-sized symphony orchestra I made one complete album of Beatles music, featuring some of the finest Lennon/McCartney hits.

I also recorded 'Two For The Road', an original score which Henry Mancini gave me, featuring Stéphane Grappelli, who played for Mancini on the version made in Hollywood for the 1967 film soundtrack. I produced a couple of recordings with Tony Bennett for his CBS LP A Time for Love. Bobby Hackett, on tour over here with Bennett at the time, played a magnificent cornet solo on one title, 'The Very Thought Of You'.

When Ashley Kozack joined my office as a booker, he was already looking after a couple of clients. Roger Whittaker comes from East Africa and has lived most of his life in England, where he became popular for writing and recording his own folk-flavoured songs and had his initial chart success in 1969 with 'The Leavin' Of Durham Town'. Donovan was an up-and-coming young folk singer and song-writer. His Dylanesque singing style endeared him to the growing number of flower-power folk-rock devotees in the midsixties. Between 1965 and 1967, Donovan's biggest record successes included 'Catch The Wind', 'Colours', 'Sunshine Superman' and 'Mellow Yellow'. He became a huge box-office attraction at home and abroad and, in my opinion, could have maintained his popularity for many more years but for his own foolishness.

**Vic sees that John Williams knows the
score**

**Tony Bennett shared Vic's love of jazz
and they got on well. Here with Eartha
Kitt, another of Vic's clients, in 1964**

Ashley proposed to continue acting as Donovan's personal manager but suggested that we should take over his agency representation.

When I went to America and arranged for Nat King Cole to do a tour for me, I knew I was breaking at long last the stranglehold held by Lew and Leslie Grade, with Harold Davison, on bringing top US entertainers to Britain. The deal with Cole, done through his manager, Carlos Gastel, was not just a feather in my cap but the turning point in my career as manager and agent.

Nat King Cole has tea with Vic at an EMI reception in London, 1963

Peggy Lee, a friend of Vic's through Leonard Feather, came over for her first UK performance in the early 1960s

Johnny Mathis in Bristol, 1962, on tour

In Grenada, Vic teaches Johnny Mathis to play golf during their holiday together in the West Indies

Vic took this picture of the Four
Freshmen doing a TV show in Munich
in 1961

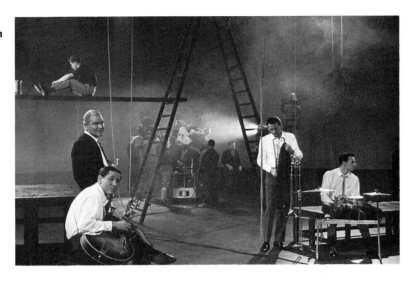

Dion (filming); facing us: Trini Lopez,
Brook Benton, Timi Yuro, Ken Thorne
and Benton's manager, at
Ross-on-Wye, 1963

Lesley Gore was also on the 1963
tour, and Quincy Jones was her
musical director

Nat King Cole was the most cooperative star I ever worked with. He was professional yet friendly, an even-tempered perfectionist – and there are not many of those around in showbiz. Nothing was too much effort for Nat. Even if I was obliged to haul him from his bed at dawn to be driven to another engagement, he never complained. He'd just drawl, 'You're the boss. You tell me what time I'm needed, Vic, and I'll be there.' Throughout his three-week tour of Britain, Nat chose to travel in my car and we got to know one another remarkably well.

Knowing the man's love of baseball, I invited him, dared him almost, to sample a small dose of English cricket at Lord's while a test match was being played. I imagined that sheer politeness might lead him to stick it out for an hour. On the contrary, he thoroughly enjoyed himself, insisted on staying all day, and ended up on the balcony of the West Indian team's dressing room. Their captain, Frank Worrell, presented Nat with a cricket ball as a memento of the visit and the singer followed the rest of that test series with much genuine enthusiasm, phoning me from all over the place to see how the West Indians were getting along.

Soon after the tour, I was in New York and made a point of dropping in to see Nat's show at the Copacabana. We had been chatting in his dressing room for some minutes when Nat said, 'Vic, you haven't noticed the difference, have you? They finally convinced me I had to stop smoking.' Sure enough, the familiar cigarette and distinctive holder were missing. A few months later, he died.

One Saturday in 1963, I was due to go up to Manchester to see Bill Benny about our next season of concert tours. By now, the Vic Lewis Organisation was presenting an inviting range of entertainers: Jeri Southern, who sang ballads in a style which kept her on the fringe of the jazz scene, best known for her version of 'When I Fall In Love'; Matt Monro; the Four Freshmen, an American close-harmony vocal jazz quartet; Kenny Baker, a fine British trumpet player; and many others. Among the new attractions I had lined up was a touring show headlined by the American pop singer Trini Lopez – who was discovered by Frank Sinatra and had a big hit that year with 'If I Had A Hammer' – supported by Brook Benton, a black American ballad singer, best known for his recording of 'Endlessly' in 1959; Dion DiMucci, who began his recording career with the Belmonts in 1959 and whose hits in the early sixties included 'Runaround Sue' and 'The Wanderer'; Timi Yuro, a white American pop singer; and old mate Ken Thorne, whose theme from the film *The Legion's Last Patrol* got to number four that summer. Bill Benny greeted me with an invitation to join him at Manchester's Free Trade Hall the same evening. 'Who's appearing?' I asked.

'I am!' came the surprise reply. Bill admitted he had been talked into taking part in a wrestling bout. He couldn't keep out of the ring although he had a weak heart. I had never seen him wrestle until that night but he was good.

In the dressing room afterwards. I warned him to take it easier. He had already complained of heart murmurings, yet he continued to weigh 20 stone, refused to slim down and still drank enormous quantities of liquids, which only made matters worse than ever. We left the Free Trade Hall and returned to the Cabaret Club, still Bill's pride and joy. After a great meal, I went back to my regular room at the Midland Hotel while Bill took a girl back to his flat to continue his partying.

At seven the next morning, I had an urgent phone call from Harold Gruber, our company's accountant. 'Vic, wake up! The worst has happened! Bill is dead! He had a heart attack during the night.' I was stunned. I really loved that man. All I could say was that if Bill had to die, this was the way he would have wished to go, in the middle of a night's lovemaking with a favourite girl.

Three days later, I attended Bill's funeral service, although I believe burial is archaic. I have not been to a graveside ceremony since my father died in 1942. People from all over Britain came to Bill Benny's funeral. As his mourners walked solemnly in silent procession through the cemetery, the heavens opened up. Watching from the doorway of the chapel, I had never seen such a torrential downpour of rain, even in Manchester. As the raindrops cascaded down the cheeks of so many of Bill Benny's best friends beside his grave, I thought to myself, Bill, you old bugger, you're a joker to the last, drenching all this lot while you stay dry.

Within less than a week, Bill's wife, Enid, contacted me to say she wanted to wind up the partnership. Her decision was a bitter blow because it left me requiring capital from a fresh partner at short notice. The Trini Lopez tour was going badly, losing thousands of pounds. My daughter's godfather, Bernie Coleman, came to the rescue. Bernie was a publican who ran jazz nights in the back rooms of his pubs. His big loves were music and cricket, a combination which cemented our friendship. He was monetary wizard of Surrey County Cricket Club and was involved with financial and promotional affairs for the Test and County Cricket Board. Thanks to his generous nature, the Vic Lewis Organisation continued to operate.

I was able to repay Bernie when I teamed up with an old friend, Allan Blackburn, the major booking agent at the time for entertainment at all the American military bases in Germany. Allan had given my band a number of dates in Germany and we had become quite friendly. Now, not long after Bill Benny's sudden death, he came to me with an intriguing partnership proposal. 'Between us, Vic, I believe we could take over UK representation of GAC.'

The General Artists Corporation of America was a giant outfit which looked after many of the world's greatest entertainers. Over the years, there had been a pretty solid association between GAC and Lew and Leslie Grade, and the possibility of breaking into that territory was one I was unable to resist. The deal we signed called for GAC to own precisely half of a company to be called the Blackburn-Lewis Agency. The Americans were to invest money in a building at 36 Curzon Street in Mayfair, our new headquarters. Whenever we booked American acts from the GAC roster, we were to credit GAC with half the agency commission we received, and when GAC booked our acts into America, we were entitled to half.

The arrangement was heavily one-sided in practice since we brought numerous Americans into Britain under the scheme but GAC took no more than a handful of our artists for dates in the US. This imbalance continued until the Beatles arrived on

Vic meets Duke Ellington backstage at the Royal Festival Hall in the early 1960s

Tony Crombie, Ray Ellington, Johnny
Dankworth, Vic, Cleo Laine, Duke
Ellington and Marion Ryan

the international scene in 1964.

The first year of the GAC association saw a great deal of business being done, even if the transatlantic traffic in talent was all in one direction. I spent several months in New York, working from the GAC offices. We brought Howard Keel to London to star in a special BBC TV gala performance of *Kiss Me Kate*, one of the inaugural programmes on the new BBC-2 channel. Good memories came flooding back in the mideighties when I began to see the charming Howard Keel in a totally different BBC TV context, as a soap-opera actor in *Dallas*.

Next came the Everly Brothers, for whom we booked concert dates in Britain and the Philippines. Then we brought over Sidney Chaplin to star opposite Barbra Streisand in the musical *Funny Girl* at the Prince of Wales theatre in the West End. Barbra came close to crossing my path again when her manager suggested that she and Donovan might join forces in the recording studio to make a special album, singing Donovan's own songs. I thought this was a superb idea. To my dismay, Donovan rejected it after minimal debate, saying, 'How can Streisand do more with my songs than I'm capable of on my own?'

During this period, a number of bandleaders I had signed up outside the GAC deal came to London to do a splendid series of television specials produced by Yvonne Littlewood, one of the finest talents in her field. She has always had a special flair for presenting orchestras to advantage on the small screen. My list

Vic with Henry Mancini in London, 1968

included Nelson Riddle, David Rose, Percy Faith and Henry Mancini.

The association with Allan Blackburn ran into trouble after a couple of years. He was devoting an increasing amount of energy to booking acts for his own shows in Germany and I found that the weight of the agency business was on my shoulders. In 1965 the title of the business reverted to the Vic Lewis Organisation. We sublet two floors of the Curzon Street building, one to the notorious Don Arden, a highly colourful music-business impresario, another to the publicist Ken Pitt, who represented Manfred Mann.

**Donovan in a Paris TV studio,
mid-1960s**

One of our major stars was Donovan, entering his period of peak popularity during the flower-power era. Donovan came from a working-class family in Glasgow. He had a superficial charm and gentleness of nature which everyone found totally disarming. It was easy to see why he and Ashley Kozack got on so well. To my mind, Kozack was never a great agent, but he shared his artist's easy-going attitude.

On our first trip to New York together, Donovan was surrounded by friends and hangers-on, holding wild all-night parties where drugs were handed round between the guests as freely as canapés at a cocktail party. I found it difficult to accept that Donovan, so concerned about healthy eating habits that he had his father travelling with us to prepare his natural-diet dishes, should fail to appreciate the dangers of drug abuse. One way and another, vast sums of money were frittered away needlessly by Donovan and his eccentric entourage. Fortunately, via Donovan's father, I was able to make the artist see better sense, if only regarding his management. In time, Ashley was persuaded to withdraw from the situation, permitting me to play a much more active role in the direction of Donovan's career, while his father assumed the nominal title of personal manager.

As we progressed through the sixties, I realised that Donovan was not the only one of his generation to experiment with drugs. I tried a few of the fat joints that were passed around from mouth to mouth beneath my nose but the stuff did little for me. I hurried back to my alcohol, needing a drink more than I ever needed marijuana. On the other hand, I don't believe I ever suggested to Donovan or the others I came across in similar situations that it was wrong to puff away at those eagerly shared joints. The choice was theirs, unless their life style affected their reliability as performers or influenced their creative powers adversely.

I found that on America's West Coast, even more than in New York City, most of the biggest names in and behind the music business enjoyed the 'high' life, popping pills and smoking pot with decreasing discretion. This must have been the first time since Prohibition that so many ordinary citizens were prepared to defy the law for the sake of pleasure.

Donovan's opening at the Hollywood Bowl was fabulous. During his act, scores of youngsters filed across the front of the seating area, flinging bunches of flowers across the stretch of water that separated the audience from the stage. Donovan sat cross-legged on a rug, wearing a long white robe and singing his peaceful folk songs.

On a later visit to LA, Donovan's promoter took over the biggest billboard site on Sunset Boulevard. Donovan spent a Sunday afternoon painting the entire hoarding by hand, watched by a crowd of thousands which stopped the Beverly Hills traffic.

I had already been friendly for some years with the film producer David Puttnam when he convinced me that Donovan should play the title role in *The Pied Piper*. He brought in a famous French director, Jacques Demy, and location shooting took place in a little German town where the buildings had been reconstructed to resemble Hamelin. Either because the film's co-star, the actor and cricket player John Hurt, was so strong, or Donovan's acting was too weak, the finished movie did little for my artist's career and he got no further major film parts.

The same year, 1972, the Italian film director Franco Zeffirelli commissioned Donovan to write the score for his new picture, *Brother Sun, Sister Moon*. During our stay in Rome, Donovan and Zeffirelli had so many rows that I feared neither the music nor the film would ever be finished. At length, when Donovan's contribution

Donovan at the Château de Chillon, Vevey, Switzerland, during the filming of *If It's Tuesday, It Must Be Belgium*, 1972

David Puttnam and Vic on the *Pied Piper* set in Germany, 1972

was complete, Zeffirelli threw a house party at his place on the outskirts of Rome. Released from the special tensions of this bizarre venture, I got extremely drunk, and Donovan hauled me home at dawn.

Donovan's professional lifespan as a popular ballad singer continued for some time after the flower-power phase had wilted away. We toured the world. His financial advisers were recommending that Donovan should base himself in America, staying out of Britain for at least one year to be exempt from tax. In Japan, Donovan had a big row with his American girlfriend, who walked out on him to return to her home-town lover. Donovan's father and I were summoned to an urgent meeting at which the artist demanded to be flown back to Britain at once. As patiently as possible, I attempted to reason with our heartbroken hero, asking him to weigh up his present misery against the devastating consequences of a trip home when the taxman would descend on him from a great height.

He only smiled his gentle smile and replied, 'I'm not interested in money, you both know that. I just want to go home now.'

His father and I spent the rest of that long night begging him to change his mind, but he flew back the next day.

At the time, I was quite convinced I would never have further professional dealings with Donovan. He married the long-term love of his life, a lady named Linda, and settled in America. But in 1981, he asked me to manage him again.

I should have asserted my feeling that it was indeed too late – too late for Donovan to revive his career and too late for me to go through it again. 'The music scene has changed, Don,' I tried to tell him. 'It's all very different today. You haven't made a record, you haven't done any television. When was your last concert?' But the temptation to tackle one last challenge before settling for the luxury of total retirement was more than I could resist. I worked out one huge publicity stunt to herald Donovan's return.

A colleague of mine, Johnny Rivers, a Polish refugee living in Rome, was visiting me at the time. Johnny's cousin was one of the Pope's private secretaries. What could be more appropriate for the pop world's former Prince of Peace than a public meeting with the Pope? I figured it had to mean front-page newspaper headlines for Donovan even at this late stage.

The rain drenched us as we stood in the square in a crowd of something like 15,000 people. The Pope made a special point of walking over to our little party and embracing Donovan as the press cameras clicked away.

For a time, it looked as though the plan to relaunch Donovan might work out. But soon he accused me of giving him insufficient attention and devoting too much of my time to watching cricket. Yet I had agreed to handle Donovan's affairs as a favour, I had earned him close on a million dollars and tied up a promising new recording deal. This rejection confirmed my blackest feelings about the entertainment business and helped to persuade me that I was better off without all that glamour and glitter and dirty tricks.

In the midsixties, I had booked a guest appearance for Donovan on the top-rated Andy Williams television show in America. From our first meeting, Andy impressed me as a decent person and as a first-class performer. He was a perfection-ist who cared not only about his singing, but also about all the other factors of a successful TV show. After each week's programme had been put in the can, Andy would call a meeting of the production team in his office to go over precise plans for the next one.

This was the beginning of a long and close relationship between us. At one stage, we discussed a plan whereby he might increase his record sales substantially on the Continent. The idea was to use my connections with the Royal Philharmonic Orchestra in London to mount a series of concert dates for Andy in the major cities of Europe, with the backing of a full symphony orchestra.

To kick off the series of shows, I arranged a charity gala concert at the Royal Albert Hall. Because the proceeds were in aid of the Save the Children fund, the charity's patron, Princess Anne, agreed to attend. During the first half, the RPO, conducted by Ken Thorne, performed the world premiere of a piece I had composed for my *Russian Suite*. I was delighted when Princess Anne turned to me in the royal box and said, 'Did you really write that music? How marvellous! It sounded so very Russian.'

While she waited to meet Andy Williams in the Albert Hall's greenroom during

Donovan, Andy Williams and Vic at the Bel Air Country Club golf course in Los Angeles, late 1960s

the interval, Princess Anne asked my wife, 'Are you as dotty about cricket as your husband is?' When Jill said she was, the princess replied, 'How fortunate for you! I can't understand why people are so crazy about chasing after a little ball.' For my part, I was so deeply enamoured with Princess Anne that I wrote something for her wedding day, entitled 'Homage To A Princess'.

Jill looks on as Vic and Princess Anne share a joke at the Royal Albert Hall, 1972

Andy Williams sightseeing in Amsterdam, 1974

Our hosts in Scandinavia did everything in their power to make Andy Williams enjoy his stay. On a night off in Denmark, it was suggested that we should drive into the heart of the countryside to dine at a most exclusive rural restaurant. Afterwards we would be taken towards Jutland, to a remote castle where a special pornographic show was staged. 'It is presented with absolute taste,' our host assured Andy.

'I daren't do this,' the singing star said, chuckling.

I told him not to be so coy. 'In the outback of Denmark, who's going to recognise you?'

But seven out of ten members of the little audience turned out to be rich American tourists who stood up and applauded Andy's entrance. And the whole erotic sequence was set to recorded vocal performances by Andy Williams. We left in haste.

Tea break

Taking tea with the royals and the Russians

IT IS WELL known among my friends in both cricket and showbiz circles that I am a fanatical tea drinker. In the days when I left home after breakfast to go to an office, I would swallow four large cups of tea first. My secretary did a survey on my in-office drinking and came up with a figure of twenty cups of tea during an average working day. She didn't include the couple I would get through over lunch. Add two or three more at home each evening and my daily intake of tea tots up to something not far short of thirty cups.

I demand my cup of tea at the end of even the most formal meal. I have been known to hand unwilling waiters a tea bag from my wallet. Restaurants will never learn to make tea properly. The pot must be scalding hot when it receives the boiling water. Chlorinated water supplies have ruined many a cuppa for me. Leaving the tea to brew, in bags or otherwise, is fundamental. The time varies with the blend, but brewing perfectly to suit individual preferences is important.

In 1970, I was asked by Lady Carolyn Townshend to line up some very special star for a big charity function at the Talk of the Town in aid of the World Wildlife Fund. She thought at least eight crowned heads of various European countries would be in the audience and it was essential to have a top name to sell the highly priced tickets. On the night, the cast list read like an international showbiz Who's Who, including Glen Campbell, Bob Hope, Margot Fonteyn and Rudolf Nureyev. Lady Carolyn's guest list made one of the most glittering groups ever assembled for such a function. Before attending the show with other members of our own royal family, the Queen and the Duke of Edinburgh gave a cocktail reception at Buckingham Palace.

Having been introduced to the Duke of Edinburgh, I was ushered into the main hall. A footman approached with an array of drinks in glasses on a tray. I don't drink before six o'clock. 'A cup of tea?' I asked tentatively. 'It is the cocktail hour, sir,' he replied with frosty dignity. 'We do not serve tea at this hour.' When I persevered, I was given tea in an anteroom.

**Vic has a tea break with Louis
Armstrong and Harry Francis of the
Musicians Union, 1956**

**Cover photo for the L P *Tea Break*,
1985: Vic, Bud Shank, Peter King,
Jiggs Whigham**

The main aim of many Americans at the Palace reception was to nick some small memento of the grand occasion. Most were forced to settle for something as unsensational as a few sheets of tissue from the royal loo, but Glen Campbell's wife managed to pocket a lovely old napkin with the initials V.R. embroidered on it.

Once I was invited to a private party at Kensington Palace, given by Princess Margaret and Lord Snowdon for Elton John and a few friends. After cocktails and a buffet-style meal, we were guided into a lounge where the princess persuaded Elton to play the piano. Everyone sat around very informally, some on big floor cushions. The pangs for a decent cuppa came over me. A footman I found in the corridor was eventually persuaded. He told me to go back into the music room and await his signal at the door. When he indicated that the brew was at hand, I was to nip outside and drink it in a secluded corner. Two of Elton's musicians, fellow fanatics over a cuppa, nearly ruined the whole thing by trying to get in on the act.

Even at the House of Lords, I managed to squeeze a pot of tea from the head waiter at the end of a dinner party there, and it almost kept me awake through the speeches.

•   •   •

In 1966, I was invited to visit Moscow by the Russian cultural attaché in London. I had been to numerous concerts of Russian classical music and had met Shostakovich, with his son Maxim, at the Royal Festival Hall. On these occasions, I met embassy people with whom I discussed the possibility of exchanging Russian and British musicians. I had the idea of setting up concerts in Eastern Europe for acts like the Beatles and Donovan. This led to a formal invitation to take a look at the Moscow music scene for myself, and to hear the big jazz orchestra they had there.

At 9.30 on my second morning in Moscow, I went to the headquarters of the cultural department for a conference with their minister and his various officials. I arrived a little early and was shown round by an English-speaking diplomat. I noticed glasses and bottles of water set out beside each place around the conference table. I told my guide that in England we welcomed visitors to our offices with the invitation to have a cup of tea before beginning any business meeting.

The minister and his men turned up promptly for our appointment. He was a dapper little man with a row of large medals. As we took our places at the table, a door opened and a procession of people entered, carrying a huge samovar, glasses, lemons and sugar. Everyone was served with tea, in the traditional Russian way. The delegates had not expected this and looked quite astonished. Then I spotted my guide beaming with delight at her handy little bit of PR work.

Samovars or ordinary pots of tea turned up wherever I went. At the Moscow State Circus, where the bears appeared to be more human than the majority of the performers, at the Bolshoi and at jazz-band rehearsals, there was always a supply of tea available for the cranky Englishman.

I was taken to hear some of Russia's most talented jazz musicians. I sat with the orchestra's manager in a large empty hall and listened while they played some Kentonesque jazz in my honour. Despite the precision of the playing, it lacked feeling. It reminded me of the way British jazz bands attempted to perform in the thirties, by merely following the written notes meticulously. In those days, few English musicians managed to mix with American jazzmen and learn about phrasing. The Russians still had the same problem several decades later. They asked me for tips while I was there and I tried hard to explain, briefly, the basic difference between trying to interpret jazz and classical music. They quizzed me about phrasing and I talked to them about keeping a tempo without letting it seem forced. Before I left, the manager presented me with an album of his orchestra's recordings.

Vic in Red Square, 1966, gathering inspiration for Russian suite

Bought and sold

Brian Epstein and the Beatles

IN THE EARLY years of my association with America's giant General Artists Corporation, they gave me little opportunity of sharing commission on the booking of British acts into their territory simply because American promoters were not all that keen to use any of the people I had on my books. The bosses at GAC were always reluctant to work on lesser-known acts, preferring to stick with the big names they could book out with minimum effort.

At that time, the biggest new phenomenon on the UK entertainment scene was a four-man pop group from Merseyside named the Beatles. I made a transatlantic telephone call to Norman Weiss, the executive who handled GAC's European affairs and a man for whom I had high professional regard. At this point, news of the Beatles' extraordinary success had not crossed the Atlantic. I told Norman I thought the group might just crack it with American kids too and the time was right for us to be first in with a tour offer. He said, 'If you really think they're going to be so enormous, Vic, why don't you go ahead and set up a meeting for me with their manager?'

Brian Epstein suggested that an imminent season of concerts at the Olympia theatre in Paris, opening on 14 January 1964, would make a perfect showcase for the Americans to see his four mop tops in action. This coincided neatly with Norman's plans because GAC looked after Trini Lopez, who was booked to appear on the same bill. In the brief interim period between my initial conversation with Weiss and his arrival in Paris, the Beatles made their first major impact on the US record charts, selling an unprecedented 250,000 copies of 'I Want To Hold Your Hand' in three days. On the eve of the Olympia dates, American sales of that single reached the 1-million mark. The reaction of French fans to the performances of the Beatles in Paris was far from sensational, but Norman Weiss was now prepared to go ahead on the evidence of the group's spectacular US record sales.

Because of my timely tip-off, Weiss was first on the scene with Brian Epstein, ahead of GAC's many New York competitors who all wanted to book the Beatles now. He tied up a deal with Epstein for the Beatles to do two shows at Carnegie Hall the following month for a fee of $7000. The New York promoter was to be Sid Bernstein, who later put on the Beatles at Shea Stadium. In addition, the group would do a concert in Washington.

Although this marked the beginning of a highly lucrative relationship between GAC and the Beatles, and I had set up each stage of the negotiations, I did not receive any commission. Weiss took the attitude that I had every right to expect my normal share but he was overruled by his colleagues in the GAC boardroom. They claimed the Beatles were booked by their own GAC man while he was in Paris with Trini Lopez. This was one of many disappointments I experienced in the sixties and seventies. The entertainment business had seemed relatively glamorous to a performing bandleader but I found agents too often concerned solely with turning a fast or even dishonest buck for themselves at the expense of associates and unfortunate artists alike.

As for Norman Weiss, he did his best to compensate me for what I lost on the Beatles in 1964 by advocating later that Brian Epstein should buy out my agency and appoint me to the board of NEMS Enterprises.

Epstein acted on that advice in 1965. He purchased the Vic Lewis Organisation and made me a director of his prosperous management, agency and show-promotion operation. I brought into NEMS all my VLO artists and became responsible for running the American side of the business. In due course, my involvement with Epstein's artists expanded. For instance, I was Cilla Black's agent for many years.

The first meeting I had with Cilla Black came soon after Brian Epstein had confessed to me that she was giving him a hard time. She wanted to broaden her horizons as an entertainer.

When I came into the picture, in 1966, Brian had made a recent TV special, *Cilla at the Savoy*, one of the first colour shows to be done in Britain by an independent production company. I thought the programme was pretty poor and I was not surprised to learn that Brian was having difficulty in selling it for decent money. I accompanied Brian when he negotiated a deal with Bill Cotton Jr for BBC TV. I remember persuading Brian to hold out for a fee of £1000 instead of only £500. Bill Cotton caved in and stood for the full amount. This was not a bad start to my working relationship with Cilla.

We made several attempts to launch Cilla in America but, alas, she was not their cup of tea. Elsewhere around the world, she went down well. Even in Singapore, where she sang in the huge cabaret suite of a hotel, she packed the place and was given a tremendous reception.

During the early years of Cilla's marriage, the friendship between us matured. Her husband and manager, Bobby Willis, and I put on a number of her shows, with great success. As an extension of this, we discussed forming a company together, but in the end Bobby decided that it was not such a good idea after all. This brought my professional association with Cilla to an end. I regret that I was not able to tie up

**Vic and Cilla at the Mount Cook
glacier, New Zealand, 1978**

**Cilla Black in Durban, South Africa,
1976**

**On tour with Cilla Black:
Vic and Cilla relax in Fiji, 1974**

**Vic was a walkover for Nancy Sinatra
in 1966**

the loose ends of one promising project, a Hollywood film based on the life story of
Gracie Fields, with Cilla playing the central character.

In 1966, Epstein brought Robert Stigwood into NEMS. Stigwood came from
Australia, where he had discovered four English boys who became the Bee Gees,
and he continued to promote their career from NEMS.

Epstein withdrew himself from routine day-to-day running of NEMS, content
to rely on Robert Stigwood's presence, and hiding himself away as far as possible
behind people like Wendy Hanson, Peter Brown and Geoffrey Ellis. Wendy
Hanson was Brian's personal secretary and did a magnificent job of wet-nursing the
Beatles, from buying perfume for their women to booking the airline tickets for

their holidays. Peter Brown was there more to serve Brian Epstein in a personal and social capacity than to work for the company or its artists. Geoffrey Ellis was a perfect gentleman, the company's legal and contracts man, who comforted Brian generously in his numerous hours of need.

In this last year of his life, after the Beatles had refused to make any more concert appearances, Epstein's personal priorities underwent drastic change. He took crucially less interest in the wellbeing of his other artists and neglected their careers to an unforgivable degree while he dosed himself with dangerous cocktails of drink and drugs to drown his business and private sorrows. He stopped coming to the main NEMS offices beside the London Palladium in Argyll Street and used only a small new private suite at Hille House in Stafford Street, Mayfair, where he hoped to avoid confrontation with either NEMS colleagues or outside associates. This made it difficult even to arrange a meeting with him.

When Epstein elevated Stigwood to joint chairman early in 1967, without consulting me or the other directors, a showdown was inevitable.

After failing to make direct contact with Brian, I went to his brother, Clive, who lived in Liverpool but happened to be visiting London with his mother, Queenie. Both Clive and Queenie were large shareholders in NEMS although they left most of the active policymaking and decision taking to Brian. When I told Clive I needed to sort things out with his brother, he took me to the Hille House hideaway and, by chance, Brian was there. I tackled him on the question of Stigwood's appointment but, as I might have anticipated, Brian flew into a furious rage.

For the sake of the young stars we were supposed to be looking after, I tried to

Vic visits Paul McCartney at work at EMI Studios in Abbey Road, London, 1972

carry on the business of NEMS Enterprises as normally as possible in thoroughly abnormal circumstances.

Ludicrous situations arose as a result of Brian's irrational and unpredictable behaviour. Shortly before my arrival at NEMS, he had bought the Saville Theatre in Shaftesbury Avenue from Bernard Delfont at what many considered to be an inflated price. A series of shows and concerts Epstein presented at the theatre lost large sums of money. Epstein liked having the Beatles, the Stones and other pop stars in his royal box each Sunday evening. The concert bills were chosen for these people rather than the public. It wasn't until he accepted my suggestions for Sunday concert stars, Donovan and the Four Tops, for instance, that the box office began to take decent money. By then it was too late. I was left with the job of sorting out a deal whereby the venue would be sold back to Delfont. The new owner switched from theatrical to cinema shows at the first opportunity.

I was with the Four Tops at the Royal Albert Hall when they were rehearsing. It was my opportunity to supervise the lighting and sound arrangements and check that everything was satisfactory before the concert. Brian arrived as we finished a run-through, entering the auditorium with his usual flourish.

I brought the Four Tops over to meet him and he made much fuss of them, shaking their hands, praising their talent and stressing how much the Beatles loved their Motown music. I had heard it all before. Then he asked them if they were happy with their deal. In itself, this was not very professional of Brian. Managers and agents take care of such business. He might have asked the artists if they were happy with their rehearsal or their hotel accommodation, but it was not tactful to talk about the finances of the tour at such a moment.

A little confused, the Four said everything was fine.

Epstein turned to me. 'Give them an extra $3000, Vic. We aren't paying them enough. They deserve a bonus.'

His grand gesture made the Four Tops think he was a wonderful and generous employer and, as he intended, it made me feel terribly embarrassed. To pay the act some extra fees if he really felt like it was Epstein's absolute prerogative. But it could have been done more discreetly.

More than once, I felt Brian was working against the interests of my side of his business. I was never any threat to his position. We were supposed to be working together to mutual advantage. He was an oddball in his personal life and in many respects a misfit in the entertainment business, surviving only because so many important people had to deal with him if they wanted his Beatles.

To be fair, Epstein could be a completely charming host when he wished to be. In the office, caught on a good day, he could also be a fair-minded negotiator who deserved his reputation for straightforward dealing and integrity. Unfortunately, he grew decreasingly reliable during the final months of his stormy life and those good days became few and far between. The pitiful problems of his personal life, the destructive anguish caused by his strange homosexual preferences, intruded on his professional activities to the detriment of his clients.

Ringo visits Vic in his office, 1967

By 1967, the Beatles were getting very heavily into the drug scene, something which Epstein was in no position to prohibit. When I accompanied Brian to the EMI Studios in Abbey Road to watch the group record, I could sense that they were going their own way. They retained a certain sentimental admiration for him as a friend and respected what he had done for them in his management capacity in the past. But he held little or no control over their music and was no longer able to make decisions about work on their behalf. Most of all, Epstein wanted his Fab Four back on the road, back on the concert stage. He made numerous attempts to get a tour organised but they remained adamant that they would never do another live show in public.

For my part, I was a late arrival on the Beatles' scene, a fresh face, which made them suspicious. Still, we got on pretty well. I became closest to Paul McCartney, with whom I had many discussions about my days as a bandleader. His father had been a bit of a jazzman and Paul remembered being brought to the Liverpool Empire as a lad in the late fifties, to watch the Vic Lewis Orchestra in action with various visiting American billtoppers. I also got on reasonably well with Ringo Starr, although we had less in common to chat about and most of our conversation was restricted to good-humoured small talk. George Harrison and I talked if he felt like it. He made it quite clear when he did not feel like it. I found it hard to communicate with John Lennon. I thought his wife, Cynthia, was a charmer and I was fond of her. But John was bitterly sarcastic on almost every occasion we exchanged words.

All four Beatles behaved peculiarly, considering the status they had achieved as entertainers and the amazing wealth they had accumulated. I expect their fans pictured the Beatles eating slap-up gourmet meals in London's poshest places every night. Far from it! Whenever I was at their recording sessions, I watched them tuck into portions of greasy fish and chips, eaten straight out of old newspapers. They sent their roadies off for this stuff when they felt peckish, and washed down the chips with Scotch and lemonade.

• • •

Over the August Bank Holiday weekend in 1967, I was playing cricket at Ashington, a small town outside Newcastle. It was a charity match for Rohan Kanhai, a great batsman who became captain of the West Indies. I had just gone in to bat on the Sunday when a man came running towards me. It was unheard of for anyone to interrupt a game by invading the field of play. As usual, my first fear was that there must have been some sort of family disaster, especially when he panted out his message, 'Mr Lewis, you're to phone your wife immediately!' I was convinced my mother or my daughter had met with a dreadful accident. I asked the umpire if I might go off and signalled to the pavilion for another batsman to be brought on.

I found a telephone and dialled our Mill Hill number. Jill was sobbing as she gave me the news. 'Brian is dead!'

'Thank God!' I said. It was an instinctive reaction when I knew that nobody truly close to me had passed away.

Jill told me that Brian had been found dead early that day in Belgravia, alone in a bedroom of his Chapel Street house. She said I was expected there for a NEMS meeting on Monday morning. There was nothing I could do by racing back to London right away.

Rohan Kanhai urged me to go back into the game. When the next player was out, he took my elbow. 'Go on, boy, set aside your grief. Get out there and play cricket.' Of course, I found it impossible to put Brian's death out of my mind. The first ball I received hit me on the pad. The umpire's finger went up and I was given 'out'. Neither he nor the rest of the fellows on the field knew my news until the innings ended. After the match, I drove back to London to keep my Monday morning appointment at Chapel Street.

My own belief is that Brian met his untimely end by accident. We shall never know the truth and I tend to write off as so much fiction the colourful versions which have cropped up in biographies of the Beatles over the years. Brian was a disturbed man, ill at ease over his business affairs and never really happy in his love life, a lonely individual despite the hordes of people who appeared to be beside him most of the time. I think he might have been able to live with himself, accept his homosexuality instead of loathing it, had he shared his time with a devoted partner in a loving relationship. As it was, love played no part in his weird life style.

Clive and Queenie Epstein offered me the post of managing director of NEMS. Meanwhile, I received a proposition from Stigwood. He invited me round to his

Vic was Nina Simone's agent for some ten years from the mid-1960s (Dezo Hoffmann)

Two of Vic's former tenor-sax players, the late Tubby Hayes and the club owner Ronnie Scott, meet Dave Brubeck in the late 1960s (Flair Photography)

**Vic with another jazz great, his old
friend Woody Herman, on a visit to the
UK in the sixties**

magnificent place in Brook Street, a house that included his business headquarters. We talked in his luxuriously appointed office on the first floor and he told me there was an equally beautiful room ready for me to occupy above this one. He didn't beat about the bush. 'I want you to move in as soon as you wish and take charge of my agency. I want to devote my own time now to the Bee Gees and to the recording side of my career.'

Stigwood's offer was tempting in the extreme but I did what I felt was the more honourable thing in the circumstances. I turned him down and took up the Epsteins' offer. This was a mistake.

My first move was a geographical one. I wanted NEMS to be based in Mayfair, not beside the Palladium in Argyll Street. With the help of the chief accountant, Martin Wesson, I found suitably stylish premises at one end of Hill Street, just off Berkeley Square. We named it Nemperor House. My second move was to generate a new image of strength and vitality at NEMS. The whole company required an injection of enthusiasm, a good kick up the backside. Under Brian Epstein's direction, the only successful part of the business was the Beatles' management. Their commission was subsidising other areas which were losing money hand over fist. Although it was well over a year since the Beatles had packed in their lucrative touring, little had been done to shore up NEMS earnings generally to compensate for this. On the contrary, heavy losses were being taken for granted. In a few short months of concentrated effort, I reversed this dangerous trend and the future was beginning to look rosier.

On one of my next trips to America's West Coast, in 1968, I was in my suite at the Beverly Hills Hotel when a call came through from Martin Wesson in London. He warned me, 'If you're standing up, I think you should take a seat. Clive Epstein has sold NEMS.'

Around the world to Watford

Coping with Elton John and the arrival of Punk rock

NEMS HAD BEEN bought by a banking firm called Triumph Investment Trust. Clive said that death duties on Brian's estate were so high that very big money had to be raised without delay. If the Epsteins had discussed the full extent of the family problem with the new NEMS board, I believe we could have found a way of raising their money without selling out and without losing the Beatles. I feel sure that EMI would have come up with the cash Clive and Queenie sought without letting NEMS pass into the hands of outsiders.

By now, the Beatles had started to fend for themselves. Although they held stock in NEMS, they wanted out. They set up their own Apple Corps concern, a group of ill-fated companies run by a pair of Liverpudlians – their former roadie Neil Aspinall and Brian Epstein's close pal Peter Brown.

Under the astute chairmanship of Tom Whyte, the Triumph people dealt strictly in financial affairs rather than theatrical or artistic matters. Once the company takeover was complete, Triumph displayed little interest in the operation of NEMS as an agency for the promotion of talent. They wanted to handle the royalties that poured in from worldwide sales of records the Beatles made. At first, I told Tom Whyte I did not wish to work for Triumph, although my NEMS contract had not run out. By his personal charm, he persuaded me to stay, but I told him bluntly that I wanted Clive Epstein out of the company.

Tom listened patiently as I outlined my terms. 'I want to be chairman of the board. I want your assurance that Triumph will let me operate NEMS without interference from the parent body.' He gave me his word.

Two very positive events occurred in 1969. The first was my purchase of a thriving contemporary-music business, the Bryan Morrison Agency, which brought under the NEMS umbrella a marvellous bunch of bands headed by the psychedelic innovators Pink Floyd and Tyrannosaurus Rex, at that time an acoustic duo of Marc Bolan and Steve Took. The acquisition of names like these did much to rebuild the reputation of NEMS within rock-music circles, proving there was life after the Beatles for our company and we were ready to move with the times.

The second shot in the arm was delivered by Don Black, now more of a partner than an assistant. In his usual persuasive but placid way, he brought me a young songwriter named Elton John. Elton played his piano for us and did some of his own compositions. I knew very quickly that Don had not exaggerated. As a songwriter, he was a potential world-beater.

'Am I right?' asked Don afterwards

Of course he was, but I wanted to be cautious. 'We need to see him at work with a band to know how he'll do in concert, Don. He needs a drummer and a bassist, at least. Then, let's see what sort of an act he can put together.'

When we came to talk seriously to Elton John about representing his interests, I found out he had already signed a contract with Dick James, the music publisher. This covered not only the publishing of all Elton's songs but also the recording side of his career. He would be with Dick's own DJM record label. The deal I worked out with Dick James was that he would assume the role of Elton's personal manager while I became the agent. We would work together very closely to plan each stage of the newcomer's future. We recognised there was a lot of work to be done to polish this absolute beginner's technique as a performing artist.

As things turned out, Elton had to prepare himself for his first stage date much faster than we intended. I was in the middle of firming up a European tour for the Brazilian bandleader Sergio Mendes and saw my chance of slotting in Elton to do the first spot on the show. I told Mendes, 'I can recommend the Elton John trio. They're brilliant!' Mendes agreed we should use the act, at a fee of £60 per night. Now we needed to form the trio.

Elton found a pair of good musicians, Nigel Olsen on drums and Dee Murray on bass. By the time they were due to open in Paris with Sergio Mendes, I thought Elton's threesome was sounding just great. Mendes thought otherwise. The morning after the Paris performance, the Brazilian rang me to complain. He paid off Elton John and sent the poor lad home in disgrace.

Once Elton John was an established star, I relished my occasional meetings with Sergio Mendes. Whenever we happened to come across each other on our travels, I would say, 'Hey! Would you like to buy another brilliant group for sixty quid a night, then?'

Dick James and I decided we should introduce Elton John to America at the first opportunity. Armed with his album, which was taking off quite nicely, I headed for California. I had formed a business relationship with Jerry Perenchio who had just left GAC, taking with him many of their artists.

Harold Davison was now with the giant London-based MAM organisation, representing stars like Tom Jones, a major attraction GAC were keen to look after for America. This was fine with Davison because it would be a two-way deal, giving him and MAM UK representation of many top American acts. This combination of circumstances led GAC to end my deal with them, and I affiliated to Chartwell, which had been set up by Jerry Perenchio and another agent, Fred Dale. Their

Elton John plays in Stockholm, 1974

partner was an Englishman, an old friend of mine, Hugh French, manager of Richard Burton and Elizabeth Taylor. Perenchio was representing Andy Williams at this time, so I was with people I felt I had every reason to trust. The Chartwell offices were located on Wilshire Boulevard and here I played my Elton John album to Howard Rose, who looked after the pop side of the firm's business.

I met with a typical American response. 'Even if the record is good, how can we sell an unknown name in this country?'

Not to be put off, I roped in the record company that represented Dick James's label in America and, between us, we lined up a one-off live appearance for Elton. The deal was with the local Troubador Club in Beverly Hills, a place which was famous for its use of English acts, including unknown groups, on special terms. If a new band hit the jackpot after a debut performance, the Troubador held an option to present them for two further appearances at a ridiculously low fee. On Elton's opening night, we had Sammy Davis Jr, Quincy Jones and Mama Cass in the audience. The trade papers gave Elton rave reviews, his record zoomed up the sales charts and our paid-off Paris flop turned into a pop sensation in next to no time. When we told the owner of the Troubador that we wanted to buy our boy out of his two additional dates, the answer was that the option would be waived only if we coughed up $100,000. This was a measure of Elton's suddenly inflated value in America.

Our newest star consolidated his stateside success with a concert in New York in front of a wildly enthusiastic audience at Madison Square Garden. Here, and at a date in New Jersey, I went on stage with Elton for his finale and played the tambourine. These shows, together with a performance at Anaheim in California, set Elton John on a smooth road to superstardom, one of the swiftest successes a British artist had enjoyed in the States since the launch of the Beatles at Carnegie Hall.

At Chartwell, Jerry Perenchio rose to become one of the most influential moguls in America's entertainment industry, selling out the agency somewhere along the way. Sadly, Hugh French died at an early age.

•   •   •

In due course, Elton took up with a chap named John Reid who was working as a label manager with EMI Records in London. Elton's temperament seemed to change for the worse during the period when his relationship with John Reid was growing close. He became difficult to deal with, causing us one problem after another. Contracts made for Elton by me or by Dick James were beginning to run out and were not renewed.

In 1974, I set up a tour of Australia and New Zealand for Elton. After the show one evening when John Reid was not around, Elton joined me for dinner and our conversation came round to cricket. Although he was interested in the game, Elton confessed that his deepest passion was for football. He was living at Rickmansworth, not far from Watford's ground, and wanted to join their board of directors. We spent a wholly pleasant evening together.

From Australia, we moved on to New Zealand. The city fathers of Auckland arranged a formal welcoming party in one of their large parks. That day, John Reid decided to go yachting and returned over half an hour late. Elton refused to leave his room until John Reid turned up.

We arrived at the park just in time to prevent the disbanding of the Maori dancers, who had come to perform a war dance. Elton entered into the spirit of the occasion magnificently, playing up to the dancers as they approached and challenged him in traditional fashion, their tongues hanging out menacingly, their spears thrust forward towards their honoured guest.

While they were waiting, journalists had kept the staff of the press bar busy. Once the big display was over, our group joined the press people and various VIP guests for drinks. Suddenly, one of the organisers tugged at my elbow. 'Get Elton John and your whole party out of here as quickly as possible. A woman reporter says Elton's manager has hit her in the face.'

I rounded up Elton, the local promoter and our various aides. As our convoy of Rolls-Royces left, the police were arriving. Back at the hotel, we pieced together the story. John Reid had become very angry with a barman when the particular drink he wanted was unavailable. It had been explained to Reid that fresh supplies were on the way. Foul language had filled the air and a woman from the press entourage turned on John Reid, saying, 'Who the hell do you think you are?' The next thing observers saw was this woman falling to the ground, blood dripping from her mouth.

The next morning, while John Reid was eating his breakfast, police arrived to arrest him. There had been a fist fight at a disco after the reception and another reporter had been punched. Reid was found guilty and sentenced to one month's imprisonment. Elton was very upset. We sought the assistance of every legal expert in Auckland but nothing could be done to quash the conviction. John Reid had to serve his time.

Back in London, I arranged a surprise for Elton. I contacted the sports editor of the *Hendon Times*, Fred Harris, and via his counterpart at Watford, a meeting was fixed for me with Watford Club's chairman, Jim Bonser.

I told Bonser how keen Elton was to become involved with the club and we agreed that having the celebrity on the board would be of obvious benefit to Watford's public image. Jim Bonser offered to discuss the idea with his directors, adding that he would like to invite me to fill another vacancy on the board so that I could accompany Elton and look after his interests generally in connection with Watford affairs. The Watford board took Bonser's advice and we received our formal invitations to become directors.

The day I took him along to Watford's ground to finalise the details, Elton was over the moon. With a grin which spread from ear to ear and back again, he told me, 'This has to be the happiest day of my life.'

Watford's finances were in the doldrums, so Elton helped to organise a fund-raising concert. Whenever our business commitments permitted, the two of us attended almost every home and away match the club team played during the next couple of seasons.

I had never been all that keen on football. Living fairly close to Watford myself, I had followed their exploits and even turned up at White Hart Lane when they played Chelsea in a cup semi-final, but seeing so much more of the game, in Elton's

**Vic with Elton John and Jim Bonser,
the chairman of Watford Football
Club, 1975 (*Watford Observer*)**

**Vic and Elton in the directors' box at
Watford F C, 1975**

company and in the intriguing role of fellow board members, made it all quite enjoyable.

One day, Elton came to me with a suggestion. 'Don't you think it would be a great idea if we got John Reid on the Watford board with us?'

My negative response was immediate and emphatic. 'Apart from anything else, he's a Scotsman, he supports St Mirren!'

Elton pressed the point. 'I know John wants to join us, Vic. I think we ought to try and use our influence . . .'

As soon as Reid was able to do so, he terminated my agency's contract with Elton. When the new football season opened, Jim Bonser asked me to resign. 'Not a single one of the directors wants you to go, but the decision is between you and Elton. The club can't afford to lose Elton John at this stage.' This was the most hurtful blow I've taken in my adult life.

Not long afterwards, Elton John replaced Jim Bonser as chairman. A little later, Bonser died.

•   •   •

As I had expected all along, Triumph Investment Trust proved to be a most unlikely parent for an entertainment agency. The City was their territory, not the recording studio, the concert stage or the television theatre. Triumph's chairman, Tom Whyte, more or less lived up to his promise to keep the parent company's nose out of NEMS' affairs.

The next buyer of NEMS Enterprises, a year or two later, was an outfit called Worldwide, controlled by a film company based in Audley Street. Martin Wesson, the NEMS money man, and Don Black survived from our old board, but not for very long.

My new chairman was Patrick Meehan, who was in charge of Worldwide's so-called light-entertainment interests. At first I believed we would get along well but our personalities clashed.

Pat Meehan was a very tall, good-looking young man in his midtwenties. His beard gave him an aura of authority and maturity. He was well educated, drove a Rolls-Royce and kept more than one luxury yacht for getaway weekends. He had a mews town house and a large place at Penshurst in Sussex. Pat had a well-trained business brain but turned very nasty when anyone threatened to tread on his toes. Pat's pet project was Black Sabbath, a heavy-metal band. With their outrageous vocalist, John 'Ozzy' Osbourne, they hit the headlines in 1970, scoring initial chart success with something called 'Paranoid' on the Vertigo record label.

Although Pat had a bit of a whiz-kid image as a high-powered music-business tycoon, he also knew how to use his time off. We went on holiday together once, taking our wives, both named Jill. The vacation began in Barbados, took in Trinidad (at test-match time, naturally) and ended with a week in Tobago. On the eve of the test, Pat put on a marvellous dinner party at the Trinidad Hilton for all

**Billy Fury and Vic clutching their feet
at the Beverly Hilton in Los Angeles,
early 1970s**

my English and West Indian cricket-playing pals, including Sir Garfield Sobers, Rohan Kanhai, Pat Pocock, Bob Willis and Geoffrey Boycott.

When my wife joined in a cricket discussion between Pocock, Willis and Boycott, Geoffrey sprang to his feet and yelled, 'Women who know nothing about the game should not gatecrash conversations regarding cricket!' His comrades rushed over and prevented further argument by removing him from the scene as swiftly as possible. 'I may not play but I've seen almost as many cricket matches as he has!' muttered Jill.

Since my early days as a musician, I had been used to planning my own professional destiny and making my own moves. At NEMS, under Pat Meehan's regime, I was never in proper control of anything, cash included. The lack of freedom in monetary matters and my constant worry over Worldwide accounting methods bothered me.

On the artistic side, Pat Meehan knew and understood the contemporary rock-music scene. My territory was middle of the road, a very different road from the one the heavy-metal bands belted down. This was the beginning of the punk-rock period, which debased the British pop industry shamefully in my eyes. Needless to say, Patrick's prime ambition was to sign the Sex Pistols.

When my mother suffered a stroke and was taken into hospital, I told Patrick that I would not be coming into the office while she was so seriously ill. I intended to spend as much time with her as she had left. In July 1977, Mum died and I never went back to the NEMS building. I quit while my personal credibility remained more or less intact, deciding to settle for independence and peace of mind.

Cricket and concertos

Retirement and After

JAZZ WENT THROUGH a period of change after 1960. In the earlier days of bebop, jazz was much influenced by Charlie Parker and Dizzy Gillespie, the two exponents who meant most to me. Their solo playing could not be bettered.

Over the years, jazz improvisation became increasing complex, emphasising the technique of a player, even to the extent of his tone. The sound was hardened as musicians relied on harmonics, as opposed to notes, for effect. They were blowing high, squeaky notes to show off their technique. This was not music to my ears. On the classical side, violin players like Heifetz or Itzhak Perlman could play any form of music – chamber music, quartet music; Perlman even plays improvised jazz. The tone of an instrument played by a classical musician would not vary at all, whatever he was doing.

I found exceptions in jazzmen like Bobby Hackett, Shorty Rogers and Bud Shank. Shank, for example, changed his ways of phrasing without changing his distinctive tone, but some of the younger newcomers squeaked and honked and created their own curious new noises. This was a different form of music altogether and the new jazz lacked melody. It was with the advent of modern jazzmen like John Coltrane that my interest in the music waned. In addition, I was unhappy about the introduction of so much electronic instrumentation, specifically the gross overuse of synthesisers.

Meanwhile, Ken Thorne and other pals had been persuading me to hear more classical music. Although in my earliest agency days I continued to be associated with a number of recording ventures in the jazz field, I started attending up to three symphonic concerts each week. I was lucky enough to meet a number of composers – not only Shostakovich but also Sir William Walton, Sir Arthur Bliss, Malcolm Arnold, Malcolm Williamson and one of my favourite people in either the jazz or classical field, André Previn. Through talking to these and other authorities, I extended my knowledge of and interest in a whole new world of music.

Through a friend at RCA I was introduced to the chairman of the Royal

William Walton and Vic, 1977

**Vic conducting the Royal
Philharmonic Orchestra at CTS
Studios in Wembley, December 1972**

André Previn and Vic, 1977

**Vic conducting an RPO rehearsal at
the Royal Festival Hall, 1985**

Last time together with Stan Kenton: Vic conducting 'Artistry In Kenton', with the R P O in London, 1975

Jill and Vic meet the Queen Mother at the R P O fortieth anniversary celebration at the Royal Festival Hall, 1976

Philharmonic Orchestra, John Lowdell, who suggested I might join the RPO Association, the orchestra's fund-raising arm. I arranged many concerts in aid of that cause, and conducted the orchestra on a total of nine albums. I was more than compensated for my time and effort when they made me an honorary life member of the orchestra. In the eighties, I have remained very closely attached to the RPO and arranged special concerts which often link jazz and classical interests.

Allyn Ferguson, a man I first met when he came over as conductor for Johnny Mathis, has shared with me over many years of close friendship his appreciation of both jazz and classical music. In 1979 he invited me to help in the formation of the New American Orchestra. In Los Angeles in 1979, Ferguson and his colleague, Jack Elliott, became deeply involved with the activities of the Foundation for Modern American Music. Backed by large American business concerns, the foundation was running the New American Orchestra for the purpose of commissioning new works by young American composers. Brilliant youngsters were being given an otherwise unavailable opportunity of getting their works performed by a symphonic orchestra with great jazz soloists like Bud Shank. Outside America this has never happened on any worthwhile scale. Elsewhere, money may be poured into exclusively classical projects, but the New American Orchestra combines classical and jazz concepts splendidly.

The premiere concert performance of the New American Orchestra was presented to the world by Quincy Jones, Henry Mancini and Johnny Mathis. Apart from some improvised jazz, the opening-night programme was made up of four pieces of new music which had been commissioned for the occasion. These included some of the loveliest 'classical jazz' music I have ever heard. The first item, 'Statements For Orchestra', was by Allyn Ferguson and featured Bud Shank and Bill Watrous. Bud and Bill also featured in 'An American Concerto' by Pat Williams. The second half opened with Jack Elliott conducting Claus Ogerman's 'Symphonic Dances' suite. He concluded the concert with 'El Gambino' by Dick Grove. Bill Watrous is well known for his phenomenal technique. These pieces were written specifically to feature Shank and Watrous. They may well end up in the libraries of many symphonic orchestras around the world.

A couple of years later, Allyn played me a remarkably exciting recording by Rob McConnell and the Boss Brass, a new Canadian jazz orchestra. This renewed my interest in big-band jazz. I began to wonder what else I had been missing. As the eighties wore on, I felt I needed to get back to either conducting or playing jazz. In particular, I wanted to return to my own special style of West Coast music.

It should have been obvious to me all along that I would form another big band sooner or later. I waited until Shorty Rogers and Bud Shank were in London and fixed a recording session, and put together a big band for the occasion. This resulted in the album *Back Again*, released on my new record label called Concept after a piece I had written half a lifetime ago for my previous big band. This label was formed with a new-found friend, Adrian Korsner. In 1985 I recruited my old friend Bud Shank, with Jiggs Whigham on trombone and Peter King on alto, and

Back Again L P cover photo: Shorty
Rogers, Vic Lewis and Bud Shank,
1984

this time we used the BBC Radio Big Band to make the album *Tea Break*. And we
intend to go on from here.

In November 1985 I promoted with Peter Bould, who used to make live
recordings of the Vic Lewis Orchestra forty years earlier, a charity gala at the Royal
Festival Hall in London on behalf of the Royal School for the Blind. Our
star-studded company included the Royal Philharmonic Orchestra with Bud
Shank, for whom I conducted, and Dizzy Gillespie. This event was attended by
Prince and Princess Michael of Kent and marked fifty years in the business for both
Gillespie and myself. For Dizzy, this appearance with the RPO represented the
fulfilment of a long-standing ambition. For me, there was the extra excitement of
having it shown on television, and it was the first time my daughter had seen me
conduct.

•   •   •

**Vic with Dizzy Gillespie during a
cricket match in London, 1984**

**Royal Festival Hall, November 1985:
Bill Holman, Dizzy Gillespie, Vic,
Bobby Lamb, Peter Bould, Manny
Albam and Bud Shank**

In 1957, a change took place in the cricketing sector of my life. The Derbyshire team told me they were coming to London to play their annual fixture at Lord's. There were no ordinary Sunday cricket fixtures or John Player League in those days. Sunday was set aside for the county beneficiary – someone who has played for a county side and given good service – to play his fund-raising benefit matches. The Derbyshire players' stay in London, with a free day on the Sunday, provided the perfect opportunity for the Vic Lewis Cricket Club to become a fully fledged team rather than a tie-swopping society. Players with three games to their credit qualified for a tie.

Our first fixture was for Arnold Hamer's benefit, at Ickenham in Middlesex. On my team were the key players from Derby, joined by show-business folk like the actors Tony Wright and Joe Lyons; Peter Lotis, brother of Ted Heath's singer, Dennis; Ronnie Verrell, the drummer from the Heath band; the singer David Hughes; and the London Palladium musical director Woolf Phillips. This was the first of hundreds of VLCC fund-raising and charity matches which were of financial help over the years to hospitals, schools for the blind and a range of other excellent causes. The Vic Lewis club was the first team formed specifically and exclusively to play for cricketers' benefits as well as charity matches.

Micky Stewart, Sir Gary Sobers, Dennis Cox and many other good friends helped put the club on its feet and secured our long-term success. Occasionally, I found myself playing for teams other than the Vic Lewis Cricket Club. One remarkable game was for the benefit of Dennis Cox, a fine Surrey player and England twelfth man.

The match was to take place at Crewe. I told my old mate Dennis that I would be travelling up to Manchester on the Saturday, because we had a show there, and I looked forward to playing the next afternoon. He rang me on the eve of the game to tell me he had broken his arm. 'Listen, old boy, you captain tomorrow!'

I told him it was ridiculous. He had most of the West Indian test players, with Gary Sobers, Reg Scarlett and Peter Lashley, from whom to pick his captain. I was speechless with pleasure when he replied, 'They would much rather you did the job.'

After arriving at Crewe in time for Sunday lunch, I went out to toss with the opposing captain, Geoff Bull. I won the toss and put his team in to bat. I had Roy Gilchrist in my side, known as the fastest thing on two legs and a potential menace to his enemies on the cricket field. In fact, he was sent home by his own team for bowling a straight-to-the-head ball, a 'beamer', to one of his own players. The game commenced at a gentle pace with Gary and Reg bowling. At the falling of the fourth wicket, the distinctive figure of Geoff Bull emerged from the pavilion.

Portly, padded, sweatered and capped, Bull strode across the field. Simultaneously, Roy Gilchrist came up to me. 'Give me the ball, skipper!'

I replied, 'I'll tell you when I want you to bowl.'

Seconds later, as he approached the batting crease, Bull said to me in a low voice, 'You won't be bowling Gilchrist, will you?'

This was becoming an annoyance. 'What's it got to do with you?'

After Bull had scored what I considered to be enough runs, I called Roy over and said, 'OK. You're on!' He told me what field he wanted set, four slips, two gullies, two leg slips, me at mid-off.

Marking out his run, Gilly nearly left the cricket field. He delivered something supersonic. Geoff Bull was fool enough to take his eye off the ball, turning round in the opposite direction to duck. Gilly's ball hit him in the kidneys and knocked him out. The belligerent bowler went charging down the wicket, bent over Bull and roared, 'Serves you fucking right!'

Gary Sobers restrained Gilly, and later, when we went in for tea, I found out why Dennis Cox had made me captain.

Geoff Bull was the local paper's cricket writer and had been giving Gilly some terrible stick, calling him a 'thrower of the ball', and this had been Gilly's frightful revenge. After some sort of first aid, Geoff was fit enough to sit on the board and have a break. No real harm had been done. As the sun set over Crewe cricket ground that Sunday, the total on the board read 191, with Gary Sobers 187, not out.

The fellow at the other end had been watching the master.

•   •   •

Vic opening the batting with Frank Worrell at Rochdale, 1955

Vic opening the batting with V. L. Manjrekar at Oldham, 1958

During the earliest heydays of the Vic Lewis Cricket Club, in the summer of 1958 and the seasons that followed, many illustrious names joined the side, including Frankie Vaughan, John Slater and Frank Holder. On one occasion, my band was playing at Nantwich in Cheshire, where the pro was G. S. Ramchand, the great Indian cricketer who eventually captained India. Ram contacted me to say he had a benefit match coming up and would like me to play in his team. On Saturday night, the band was playing in Kirkcaldy, north of the Forth Bridge. On Sunday night, we had a pair of concerts to give in Harrogate. Nevertheless, I told Ram I would open the batting for his side. This necessitated a 600-mile drive, from Scotland to Cheshire and on to Yorkshire. But there I was in Nantwich, opening the innings with V. L. Manjrekar.

The following week, Ram invited me to go to a game in Sale, outside Manchester, where he was playing in a team which included the great Sir Frank Worrell and Everton Weekes. I could hardly believe my good luck. Without waiting to consult my diary of band bookings, I promised to come to Sale on the Sunday afternoon.

As I walked through the gates to the pavilion, I was met by two grinning heroes of mine, Worrell and Weekes, who were keen to talk jazz. Everton said, 'We saw you in Blackpool a fortnight ago.' Frank asked if the band could play at their university dance. This marked the beginning of a bond of warm friendship with the whole West Indies team.

I played in one match at Rochdale, for Datu Phadkar, against Polly Umrigar's XI. Opening the batting with Frank Worrell, the pair of us put on 74 runs for the first wicket: Worrell, 64, and Lewis, 10.

In 1958, we invited Lord Edward Montagu of Beaulieu to be president of the Vic Lewis Cricket Club. This came about when my orchestra appeared at the Beaulieu Jazz Festival that summer. I suggested to Monty the idea of having a cricket match in the afternoon before the music was due to begin. He agreed to this very readily and put together a team consisting, mainly, of men who worked in his motor-car museum or elsewhere on the Beaulieu estate. My side was made up of musicians from the many jazz-festival bands. I wrote two pieces in honour of that occasion, 'Monty' and 'Lady Belinda'. His lordship continues to hold the presidency of the VLCC at the time of writing.

One delightful incident I like to recall took place when my side was not doing too well. I was sitting in the pavilion with Gerald Lascelles, the Queen's cousin, when our batsman hit a magnificent straight drive for four. 'Who was that?' asked Lascelles.

'Bernie Coleman,' I replied.

He pretended to recognise the name of the publican and jazz enthusiast at once. 'Coleman! Ah, yes! Coleman, of course.' I am dashed if he knew who Bernie was, but the story was worth a few pints to Bernie when he related it to friends.

The vice presidency has been held by only ten players. The first was His Highness the Maharajah of Baroda, who turned out for my side during the early

Vic, Glenn Turner, Pat Pocock, Fred
Titmus and Rohan Kanhai in Bombay,
India, 1981

Flanked by Martin Weston and V. A.
Holder, Vic hits a square drive for four
off the bowling of Norman Gifford at
Glenn Turner's benefit at Worcester,
1976

days. Gary Sobers was in my team at that time, and the ex-Surrey player Dennis Cox was my vice captain. We played a match for the British Legion at Surbiton. I introduced the maharajah to each player – 'This is His Highness' etc. Dennis Cox said afterwards, 'Vic, we can't call him that on the field, surely. Hasn't he a nickname?' The problem was solved soon enough, at least in Cox's eyes. The cover drive ball reached His Highness and he proceeded to misfield it. The ball went through his legs for four and Dennis came over to me. 'Now I know what to call him. Prick!' But our vice president rallied to the cause when we batted, hitting thirty-plus runs.

Another vice president was the Hollywood actor Boris Karloff, with whom I became friendly at the Oval. He was a great Surrey supporter and let it be known in movie-studio circles that his contracts must never entail shooting a picture during the summer months. He insisted on returning to England for the cricket season. Karloff's playing days were over, but he acted as our umpire on a number of occasions and nobody argued with the decisions of Frankenstein's monster.

Our remaining vice presidents were all cricketers: Sir Frank Worrell, Everton Weekes, Sir Garfield Sobers and Rohan Kanhai, all of the West Indies; Keith Miller, that great Australian all-rounder; Mushtaq Mohammed of Pakistan; Fred Titmus, my colleague from Middlesex and England; and Glenn Turner, from New Zealand.

When I took my World XI team to play Barnet in 1960, for the benefit of Tom Clark, the opening batsman for Surrey, I captained a side that consisted of Sobers, Kanhai and Dewdney of the West Indies, John Waite, Hugh Tayfield and Roy McLean of South Africa, Micky Stewart, Ken Barrington, Jim Parks and Freddy Truman of England, with Roy Castle as twelfth man.

Being from South Africa, Roy McLean was very unlikely to have another opportunity to bat with Sobers, and he asked me if it was possible to put him in where he might get a strike with the great Sir Garfield. I decided to open with Stewart and Barrington, putting in Sobers at three and McLean at four. The first wicket fell, and in went Sobers. The second fell, and McLean was in next. Roy was clean bowled, first ball, and a noble partnership came to an untimely end even as it started.

In 1961, I repeated the fixture, again with Sobers and McLean in a slightly different side. Roy McLean was over here with a team called the Fazellas. He pleaded again to go in with Sobers, promising, 'I won't let you down this time, skipper.' He was a magnificent player, and this time he scored a ton in just over forty minutes.

Those were the great days of Sunday cricket. They had to go by the board with the advent of league matches. But I still field a pretty good side, when asked to, particularly if Sobers is around and can bring himself to exchange the golf club for the cricket bat.

•　　•　　•

My zeal for adding fresh ties to my vast collection continued. In 1974, I was in South Africa and found I had the pleasing opportunity of watching the Derek Robbins XI. A senior airline pilot gave a party for the team and, during the proceedings, the conversation turned to my habit of collecting cricket-club ties as I toured around the world. My host, a Sabena man, asked if I had a Belgian tie. I replied, 'Do they *have* a cricket team in Belgium?' He said he was their team captain and showed me a green tie with tiny Manikin Pis all over it.

Before we parted, he asked me when I was leaving, and I told him my flight details. On the homeward journey to London, my plane touched down to take on fuel at Luanda airport. When we had taxied towards the terminal buildings, and the steps were lowered, my Sabena cricketer was standing there clutching a tie. He had brought a flight into Angola about thirty minutes before. I was just as diligent about sending him one of mine.

If my fame as a cricket player never did reach the heights, I managed to achieve an associated first in the field. At the time of writing, I am the only author to have published a book devoted exclusively to cricket-club ties. From my collection of over 4000 ties, I selected several hundred of the most important and wrote the story that went with each one. Since the book's publication in 1984, I have received many letters from readers all over the world, and ties galore, accompanied by background data on each source. It has been a revelation to me to discover the extent of the interest in such a specialist subject.

●　　　●　　　●

The show-business celebrities who have played in my team hail from all departments of entertainment. A side I fielded at the Oval in 1972, for instance, included Michael Parkinson, Roy Castle, John Hurt, Michael Aspel, John Alderton, Ray Barrett, Micky Stewart, Gerald Harper and Gerry Marsden. Making his first appearance on a cricket field with me on that occasion was Andy Williams. Another typical team, which played at Lord's in 1973, consisted of Brian Rix, Elton John, Michael Parkinson, Peter Cook, Ed Stewart, Nicholas Parsons, Ray Barrett, Gerald Harper, Malcolm McFee, Malcolm Roberts and David Frost. I was also joined by Wes Hall, of the West Indies, and Dennis Cox.

Between 1956 and 1984 we had only two umpires, Dr Crock, a famous comedy bandleader, followed by Len Morris, a businessman. I could always count on these two gentlemen to give a fair decision in our favour.

Many county players who played for the side were joined by cricketers from overseas, whenever they were free for a game. Jack Bailey, now secretary of the MCC and ICC, once played against us and the score card read, 'Garfield Sobers bowled Bailey, J.' This made Jack feel ten feet taller. Mind you, the card also recorded that Sobers scored 109.

Pete Murray, the disc jockey and presenter, was an early stalwart of the side, but he preferred tennis. We had Freddie Truman and Brian Statham, the great

1973 cricket team at Lord's, back row:
Brian Rix, Elton John, Michael
Parkinson, Peter Cook, Ed Stewart,
Nicholas Parsons, Ray Barrett; front
row: Gerald Harper, Malcolm McFee,
Dennis Cox, Vic, Wes Hall, David Frost

Vic has lent his Cross Arrows cricket
cap to Jayne Mansfield, 1958

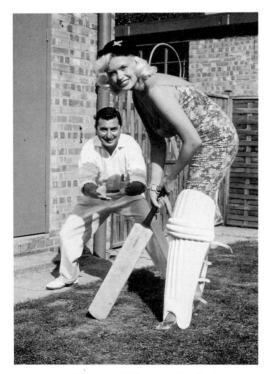

A life's ambition: leading the team out
at Lord's, 1973

The Vic Lewis Cricket Club vs Hampshire, 1977, back row: Kepler Wessels (Sussex, Queensland and Australia), John Snow (England/Sussex), David English (actor), C. S. Serjeant (Australia), Tom Baker (actor); front row: John Alderton (actor), Rodney Marsh (Australia), Vic, Malcolm McFee (actor), Tom Adams (actor), Andy McFee (actor)

The Vic Lewis Cricket Club vs Blackpool, c. 1958, back row: Hanif Mohammad, unidentified, Bernard Bresslaw, Teddy Johnson, Sid Maurice, unidentified; front row: Jim Laker, Dennis Cox, Vic, Squadron Leader Maurice Fenner, Harry Secombe

Fred's bowling partner. From music circles, we had Johnny Dankworth and Benny Green. We had Cardew Robinson, Ian Carmichael, Oliver Reed, Robert Powell, Ronnie Corbett, Dudley Moore, Harry Secombe, Dennis Waterman, Ernie Wise and George Best.

When we played against Sussex at Hove, for the bowler John Snow's benefit, Tony Gregg hit a blow that promised to send the ball all the way to the pavilion. Suddenly, a single hand went up and held a ball which not one in a thousand players would have caught. Nonchalantly, Phil Everly, of the Everly Brothers, threw the ball back. I told him frankly, 'Phil, you play better than you sing!' Playing baseball, he must have become an accomplished catcher. He loved cricket and fitted in as many games as he could when he came to Britain on tour.

I had to twist his arm, but Tommy Steele joined us for a game we played in Surrey. I thought he was joking when he tried to convince me he had never played cricket in his life. He was dreadfully afraid of being hit by the ball. That day, our side included Trevor Goddard, the South African opening bat and bowler. When we were fielding, I decided to put Tommy Steele in positions as far as possible from the batsmen. Despite this tactic, every time a batsman hit the ball, it sought out Steele. The first time a ball reached him, he picked it up and yelled to me in panic, 'What do I do with it now?' Meanwhile twelve runs were being scored.

'Throw it in!' I screamed.

'In where?'

Politeness to such a distinguished guest star prevented me from making the obvious suggestion.

Other stalwarts of the side included Julian Holloway, son of Stanley, a player good enough to have made a name for himself as a cricketer. In later years, Andy McFee, brother of Malcolm, helped to run the club when my business commitments became crucial. Andy's wife, Joan, assisted too. Reg Scarlett, the former West Indian and Jamaican test player, took over the mantle of vice captain, with Malcolm McFee, and eventually became captain. Others who turned out consistently included, from the acting profession, Christopher Blake, Jeremy Bullock, Peter Davidson, David English and Rudolph Walker. The list also included Alan Burridge, Hindie Clarke, Tony Gooding, 'Little Bird' Johnson, David Wilkinson and Dr Richard Wise, who loved to claim he was from *Doctor Who*. Apart from George Best, my footballers included Mike England, Cyril Knowles and Billy Wright.

Our opponents were many and various. We played against sides from the royal household at Windsor (who have now made me an honorary member of their number), the Metropolitan Police, the fire brigade, the houses of Lords and Commons and Barclays Bank. By the time my team was officially disbanded, at the conclusion of the 1984 season, the Vic Lewis Cricket Club must have raised well over £3 million for charitable causes. I have fielded occasional sides since then, for special games.

Today, my role in cricket is quite different. Since 1976, I have served on the

The Vic Lewis Cricket Club vs Warwickshire, 1975, back row; Len Morris (umpire), John Alderton (actor), Julian Holloway (actor), Michael Parkinson (TV presenter), Robert Powell (actor), Keith Boyce (West Indies), Fred Harris (sports journalist), Laurie Henbest (Australia), Ivor Salter (actor); front row: Dennis Cox (Surrey), Sir Garfield Sobers (West Indies), Vic, Malcolm McFee (actor), Micky Stewart (England's manager)

Vic with Andy Roberts (West Indies) and Barry Richards (South Africa)

Viv Richards and Vic tossing up at Richards's benefit at Lincoln, 1982

membership, finance, development and general committees of Middlesex Cricket Club at Lord's. The administrative meetings take up a great deal of my time the year round. My committee colleagues have included such illustrious men as Gubby Allen and George Mann, our president, a former captain of England and Middlesex. We have spent much time seeing the Second XI of the county, young players such as Norman Cowans, Wilf Slack, Neil Williams and Colin Metson. It is stimulating to meet such youngsters as they emerge from school, and to follow their progress until they are playing for the county or even for their country.

I must pay special tribute to the Cross Arrows, the side that plays on the nursery end at Lord's the day after cricket stops on the main arena at the end of each season. They continue until the last day of September. I have been playing for the Cross Arrows since the midfifties, alongside stars like Dennis Compton, Trevor Bailey, Fred Titmus, Mark Nicholas, Asif Din and many others.

I am proud to have been elected a member of the Cross Arrows, and to have been permitted to play on a few occasions for the MCC in their out fixtures. I remain a member of the Lord's Taverners, the World Wildlife Cricket Club, the XL Club, the Cricketers' Club of London, the Somerset Wyverns, Fenners at Cambridge, the Barbados Cricket Association and the Wanderers in Barbados. I have played for some of these clubs.

In 1980, I was invited to represent the USA at the International Cricket Conference, the ruling body of the game throughout the world. The offer came from their president, Naseeruddin Khan. As a rule, each of the associate members of the ICC, except those in nearby European countries, appoints an Englishman, or one of their own countrymen who lives in the UK, to be a permanent representative. This saves travel expenses for conference delegates. There are seven major countries and eighteen associates involved. I have relished this responsibility and hope to continue serving in the same capacity for many years to come.

Our team in America has gone from strength to strength. Long gone are the days when people thought cricket in America was played only in Hollywood and by C. Aubrey Smith's XI. As it happens, the first test match in the world took place between Canada and America in 1844, and the first test in which England played was at Hoboken, New Jersey, in 1859. There were over 100 cricket teams in the Philadelphia area alone in the 1800s.

I have been fortunate enough to manage my own World XI to India on two occasions, to Pakistan for a series of three five-day tests and three one-day international matches, to Dubai, Bahrein, Finland, Holland and Eire.

I seem to have travelled almost as much in my cricketer's role as I did in the old bandleading days. In 1984 I took the USA side to Barbados, where we watched the rain fall for an entire week and beat the police, said to field the strongest side on the island. Gary Sobers looked up at me and said, 'I really didn't think they were as good as this!'

It is a shame that neither my father nor my brother, Laddie, came to see me play cricket. I know Dad would have been very proud. Laddie died of a heart attack in 1957. My wife Jill, my mother and my cousin Bessie attended every match from the fifties onwards. Later my daughter joined them. Even when my mother was ninety-two years old, she refused to miss a game. If I had misfielded a ball she would say, in her true Victorian fashion, as I came in for tea, 'I don't think you fielded so well today, Victor.' Only my mother, and Nelson Riddle, used to call me Victor.

To me, cricket is not just another sport. Cricket is a religion, a way of life, a brotherhood. If only the politicians would keep their noses out of cricket, I believe the world would be a more peaceful place. 'Play the game' is an expression from cricketing jargon way back when. Long may both the motto and the game remain integral parts of the great British tradition!

Vic's mother watching cricket with Bobby Butlin, Sandy Dennis and Gerry Mulligan at Mill Hill Village Cricket Club, 1957

Full discography,
including broadcasts,
available from
MICROGRAPHY
The Golden Age Records
Nieuwezijds Voorburgwal 51–53
NL-1012 RD Amsterdam
The Netherlands

Notes

All venues/locations are London,
England, except where noted.

compiled by
TONY MIDDLETON

Abbreviations:

arr	arranger
as	alto saxophone
b	bass
bs	baritone saxophone
btb	bass trombone
cl	clarinet
cn	cornet
cond	conductor
d	drums
dir	director
elb	electric bass
fl	flute
flh	flugelhorn
frh	french horn
g	guitar
ldr	leader
p	piano
perc	percussion
ss	soprano saxophone
tb	trombone
tp	trumpet
tu	tuba
ts	tenor saxophone
vcl	vocal
vibes	vibraphone
vln	violin
vtb	valve trombone

Discography

Vic Lewis and Carlo Krahmer band

Thursday, 30 June 1938

Leslie 'Jiver' Hutchinson, *tp*; George Chisholm, *tb*; Bertie King, *cl*, *as*; George Shearing, *p*; Vic Lewis, *g*;
Joe Muslin, *b*; Carlo Krahmer, *d*.

I AIN'T GOT NOBODY	Lincon Rhythm Style No. 15, Harlequin HQ 3012
SHINE ON HARVEST MOON	Lincon Rhythm Style No. 16, Harlequin HQ 3012
ANGRY	Lincon Rhythm Style No. 17, Harlequin HQ 3012
STOOGE BLUES	Lincon Rhythm Style No. 18, DJM SPECB 103 HQ 3012

Vic Lewis and his American jazzmen

NYC, *Wednesday, 5 October 1938*

Bobby Hackett, *cn*; Dave Bowman, *p*; Eddie Condon, *g*; Vic Lewis, *g*; Zutty Singleton, *d*.

EARLY RISING BLUES	Esquire 10-230, ESQ 313
NEW YORK BLUES	Esquire 10-230, ESQ 313

Vic Lewis, *cn*; Eddie Condon, *p*; Dave Bowman, *p*; Bobby Hackett, *g*; Zutty Singleton, *d*, *vcl*.

HACKETT PICKING BLUES -*vzs*	Esquire 10-246, ESQ 313

Bobby Hackett, *cn*; Joe Marsala, *cl*; Dave Bowman, *p*; Vic Lewis, *g*, *vcl*; Eddie Condon, *g*; Zutty
Singleton, *d*.

BABY WON'T YOU PLEASE COME HOME -*vVL*	Esquire 10-246, ESQ 313
KEEP SMILING AT TROUBLE	Esquire 10-221, ESQ 313 IAJRC 38
SUGAR	Esquire 10-221, ESQ 313, DJM SPECB 103

Vic Lewis and his American jazzmen

NYC, *Wednesday, 19 October 1938*

Bobby Hackett, *cn*; Brad Gowans, *vtb*; Pee Wee Russell, *cl*; Bernie Billings, *ts*; Ernie Caceres, *bs*; Dave
Bowman, *p*; Vic Lewis, *g*; Eddie Condon, *g*; Zutty Singleton, *d*; Josie Carole, *vcl*.

TIGER RAG	Esquire 10-251, ESQ 313
LEADERS HEADACHE BLUES -*vJC*	Esquire 10-251, ESQ 313
BASIN STREET BLUES	Esquire 10-241, ESQ 313, DJM SPECB 103

George Wettling, *d*, replaces Singleton.

WRAP YOUR TROUBLES IN DREAMS	Esquire 10-241, ESQ 313
THAT'S A PLENTY	Esquire 10-231, ESQ 313
MUSKRAT RAMBLE	Esquire 10-231, ESQ 313

Jam session at Levy's

12 December 1942
Jimmy McMillian, *tp*; Don Macaffer, *tb*; Buddy Featherstonhaugh, *ts*; Jimmy Skidmore, *ts*; Harry Hayes, *as*; Harry Rayner, *p*; Vic Lewis, Ken Sycora, *g*; Frank Clark, *b*; Jack Parnell, *d*.

ANGRY	Harlequin HQ 3012
SQUATTY ROO	Harlequin HQ 3012

Jam session at Levy's

Private recordings, Levy's Studios, Tuesday, 2 March 1943
Neal Eldon, *cn*; Don Macaffer, *tb*; Buddy Featherstonhaugh, *cl, ts*; Harry Rayner, *p*; Vic Lewis, *g, vcl*; Sam Molyneaux, *b*; Jack Parnell, *d*.

JAZZ ME BLUES	Harlequin HQ 3012
THE BLUES Part 1 -*vVL*	Harlequin HQ 3012
THE BLUES Part 2	Harlequin HQ 3012

Vic Lewis and Jack Parnell's jazzmen

Saturday, 12 February 1944
Billy Riddick, *tp*; Ronnie Chamberlain, *as, ss*; Derek Hawkins, *as, cl*; Dick Katz, *p*; Vic Lewis, *g, vcl*; Charlie Short, *b*; Jack Parnell, *d*.

JOHNNY'S IDEA	CE 11197	Parlophone R 2933
MEAN OLD BED BUG BLUES -*vVL*	CE 11198	Parlophone R 2933
JAZZ BAND JUMP	CE 11199	Parlophone R 2939
I'M COMING VIRGINIA	CE 11200	Parlophone R 2939

Vic Lewis jam session

Star Sound Studios, Friday, 10 April 1944
Billy Jones, *tp*; Jake Koven, *tp*; George Chisholm, *tb*; Johnny Mince, *cl*; Joe Gudice, *ts*; Dick Katz, *p*; Vic Lewis, *g*; Charlie Short, *b*; Jack Parnell, *d*.

JOHNNY'S IDEA	Harlequin HQ 3008
WIGMORE BLUES parts 1 & 2	Harlequin HQ 3008
JA DA	Harlequin HQ 3008
WIGMORE JUMP	Harlequin HQ 3008
TEA FOR TWO parts 1 & 2	Harlequin HQ 3008
AIN'T MISBEHAVING	Harlequin HQ 3008
MY BLUE HEAVEN	Harlequin HQ 3008
SOMEDAY SWEETHEART	Harlequin HQ 3008

Vic Lewis and Jack Parnell's jazzmen

Friday, 9 June 1944
Billy Riddick, *tp*, melophone; Ronnie Chamberlain, *as, ss*; Derek Hawkins, *as, cl*; Dick Katz, *p*; Vic Lewis, *g, vcl*; Lou Nussbaum, *b*; Jack Parnell, *d*.

JAZZ MEN BLUES	CE 11243	Parlophone R 2944
JA DA -scat *vVL*	CE 11244	Parlophone R 2944
WHY BEGIN AGAIN	CE 11245	Parlophone R 2949
SUGAR	CE 11246	Parlophone R 2949
I'VE FOUND A NEW BABY	CE 11247	DJM SPECB 103

Vic Lewis and Jack Parnell's jazzmen

Wednesday, 29 August 1944
Billy Riddick, *tp*, melophone; Ronnie Chamberlain, *as, ss*; Derek Hawkins, *as, cl*; Dick Katz, *p*, celeste (on -*c* only); Vic Lewis, *g, vcl*; Bert Howard, *b*; Jack Parnell, *d*.

THAT'S A PLENTY	CE 11269	Parlophone R 2953
UGLY CHILD -*vVL*	CE 11270	Parlophone R 2960
DICK'S BOOGIE	CE 11271	DJM SPECB 103
MOP MOP	CE 11272	DJM SPECB 103

Vic Lewis and Jack Parnell's jazzmen

Tuesday, 24 October 1944
Billy Riddick, *tp*; Ronnie Chamberlain, *as, ss*; Cliff Townshend, *as, cl*; Dick Katz, *p*; Vic Lewis, *g, vcl*; Bert Howard, *b*; Jack Parnell, *d*.

IS YOU IS OR IS YOU		Parlophone R 2953
AIN'T MY BABY -*vvl*	CE11287	
GET HAPPY	CE11288	Parlophone R 2965
INDIANA	CE11289	Parlophone R 2960
SOMEDAY SWEETHEART	CE11290	Parlophone R 2965

Vic Lewis jam session

1944
Kenny Baker, *tp*; Don Macaffer, *tb*; Derek Hawkins, *as*; Buddy Featherstonhaugh, *ts*; Harry Rayner, *p*;
Vic Lewis, *g*; Charlie Short, *b*; Jack Parnell, *d*.

HONEYSUCKLE ROSE	Harlequin HQ 3012

Vic Lewis and Jack Parnell's jazzmen

BBC *General Overseas Services broadcast, 'Swing Session', Tuesday, 13 February 1945*
Billy Riddick, *tp*; Ronnie Chamberlain, *as, ss*; Derek Hawkins, *as, cl*; Laddie Busby, *tb*; Dick Katz, *p*;
Vic Lewis, *g, vcl*; Bert Howard, *b*; Jack Parnell, *d*.

I AIN'T GONNA GIVE NOBODY MY JELLY ROLL	Harlequin HQ 3010
SINGING THE BLUES	Harlequin HQ 3010

Jazz is where you find it

AEF *broadcast, Monday, 12 March 1945*
Kenny Baker, *tp*; Arthur Mouncey, *tp*; Laddie Busby, *tb*; Woolf Phillips, *tb*; Ronnie Chamberlain, *cl, as, ss*; Derek Hawkins, *cl, as*; Aubrey Frank, *ts*; Pat Dodd, *p*; Vic Lewis, *g*; Lauderic Caton, *g*; Joe Nussbaum, *b*; Carlo Krahmer, *d*; plus guest musicians from the US Navy Band: Johnny Best, *tp*; Tak Takvorian, *tb*; Ralph LaPolla, *cl*; Sam Donahue, *ts*; Rocky Coluccio, *p*.

YELLOW DOG BLUES	Harlequin HQ 3008
BLUES IN E (guitar duet)	Harlequin HQ 3008

Vic Lewis jam session

Star Sound Studios, Monday, 12 March 1945
Johnny Best, *tp*; Stéphane Grappelli, *vln*; Ronnie Chamberlain, *as, ss*; Vic Lewis, *g*; Tommy Bromley, *b*;
Carlo Krahmer, *d*.

IT'S THE TALK OF THE TOWN	Harlequin HQ 3009

omit Ronnie Chamberlain, Stéphane Grappelli plays *p*

I NEVER KNEW	Esquire ESQ 306

same as -*a*

I FOUND A NEW BABY	Esquire ESQ 306

same as -*a*, add Derek Hawkins, *cl, as*

TRI-COLOUR BLUES	DJM SPECB 103, Harlequin HQ 3009

Vic Lewis trio/jam session

Wednesday, 15 March 1945
Johnny Best, *tp*; Vic Lewis, *g*; Bert Howard, *b*.

JOHNNY'S BLUES	DJM SPECB 103, Harlequin HQ 3009

Johnny Best, *tp*; Laddie Busby, *tb*; Ronnie Chamberlain, *cl*; Aubrey Frank, *ts*; Gerry Moore, *p*; Vic
Lewis, *g*; Bert Howard, *b*; Carlo Krahmer, *d*.

MEAN TO ME	Harlequin HQ 3009
DOWN BY THE OLD MILL STREAM	Esquire ESQ 306
ROSETTA	Esquire ESQ 306

Vic Lewis jam session

February 1945
Don Jacoby, *tp*; Harry Roche, *tb*; Ronnie Chamberlain, *cl, as*; Derek Hawkins, *cl*; Sam Donahue, *ts*;
Rocky Coluccio, *p*; Vic Lewis, *g*; Bert Howard, *b*; Carlo Krahmer, *d*.

SAMS BLUES	Harlequin HQ 3009
SAMS BLUES (fast)	Esquire ESQ 306
SAMS BLUES (slow) -1	Harlequin HQ 3009
SAMS BLUES (slow) -2	Harlequin HQ 3009

LADY BE GOOD		Harlequin HQ 3009
ROSE ROOM		Harlequin HQ 3009
GHOST OF A CHANCE		Harlequin HQ 3009

Vic Lewis and Jack Parnell's jazzmen

Monday, 19 March 1945
Billy Riddick, *tp*; Laddie Busby, *tb*; Ronnie Chamberlain, *cl, as, ss*; Derek Hawkins, *cl, as*; Dick Katz, *p*; Vic Lewis, *g, vcl*; Bert Howard, *b*; Jack Parnell, *d*.

AT THE JAZZ BAND BALL	CE 11358	DJM SPEC B 103
ROYAL GARDEN BLUES	CE 11359	DJM SPEC B 103
SINGING THE BLUES	CE 11360	Parlophone R 2975
PRINCE OF WAILS	CE 11361	Parlophone R 2975, BBC Records REC 144 M

Vic Lewis and his jazzmen

Friday, 20 July 1945
Billy Riddick, *tp*; Frank Osborne, *tb*; Ronnie Chamberlain, *cl, as, ss*; Jimmy Skidmore, *ts*; Ken Thorne, *p*; Vic Lewis, *g*; Bert Howard, *b*; Harry Singer, *d*.

FIDGETY FEET	CE 11420	DJM SPEC B 103
DIPPERMOUTH BLUES	CE 11421	Parlophone R 2986
BLUIN' THE BLUES	CE 11422	DJM SPEC B 103
BALLIN' THE JACK	CE 11423	Parlophone R 2986

Vic Lewis and his jazzmen

BBC Light Programme broadcast, Wednesday, 8 August 1945
Billy Riddick, *tp*; Laurie Clarke, *tb*; Ronnie Chamberlain, *cl, as, ss*; Jimmy Skidmore, *ts*; Ken Thorne, *p*; Vic Lewis, *g*; Bert Howard, *b*; Harry Singer, *d*.

RIVERBOAT SHUFFLE; PEG OF MY HEART	Harlequin HQ 3010

Vic Lewis and his jazzmen

BBC Light Programme broadcast, Wednesday, 22 August 1945
Billy Riddick, *tp*; Jimmy Wilson, *tb*; Ronnie Chamberlain, *cl, as, ss*; Jimmy Skidmore, *ts*; Ken Thorne, *p*; Vic Lewis, *g*; Bert Howard, *b*; Harry Singer, *d*.

ROUND ABOUT EIGHT;	Harlequin HQ 3010
ETUDE IN RED;	Harlequin HQ 3010
FIDGETY FEET;	Harlequin HQ 3010

Vic Lewis and his sextet

Private recordings, Saturday, 5 January 1946
Jimmy Wilson, *tb*; Ronnie Chamberlain, *cl, as, ss*; Jimmy Skidmore, *ts*; Ken Thorne, *p*; Vic Lewis, *g*; John Quest, *b*; Tony Lytton, *d*.

N.R.C. JUMP	Boosey & Hawk No. 1, Harlequin HQ 3012
EAGER BEAVER	Boosey & Hawk No. 3, Harlequin HQ 3012
SERGEANT ON A FURLOUGH	Boosey & Hawk No. 4, Harlequin HQ 3012

Vic Lewis jam session

Sunday, 6 January 1946
Jimmy McPartland, *cn*; Clarence Magnusson, *cl*; Ronnie Chamberlain, *as*; Jimmy Skidmore, *ts*; Marion McPartland, *p*; Vic Lewis, *g*; Ken Batchelder, *b*; Joe Nardy, *d*; Grace Scott, *vcl*.

I'VE FOUND A NEW BABY	Harlequin HQ 3010
THE WORLD IS WAITING FOR THE SUNRISE	Harlequin HQ 3010
SWEET LORRAINE -*v*GS	Harlequin HQ 3010

Jimmy McPartland, *cn*; Clarence Magnusson, *cl*; Ronnie Chamberlain, *as*; Jimmy Skidmore, *ts*; Jerry Schwartz, *p*; Vic Lewis, *g*; John Quest, *b*; Tony Vitale, *d*.

JAZZ ME BLUES	Harlequin HQ 3010

Marion McPartland, *p*; Vic Lewis, *g*; John Quest, *b*; Tony Vitale, *d*.

I GOT RHYTHM	Harlequin HQ 3010

Also recorded by one of the above combinations

BLUES	Harlequin HQ 3010
ROSE ROOM	Harlequin HQ 3010

Vic Lewis and his jazzmen

Monday, 28 January 1946

Reg Arnold, *tp*; Jimmy Wilson, *tb*; Ronnie Chamberlain, *cl, as, ss*; Jimmy Skidmore, *ts*; Ken Thorne, *p*; Vic Lewis, *g*; John Quest, *b*; Harry Singer, *d*.

SRUT MISS LIZZIE	CE	DJM SPECB 103
TIN ROOF BLUES	CE	DJM SPECB 103
SMOKEY MOKES	CE	DJM SPECB 103
PANAMA	CE	DJM SPECB 103

Vic Lewis jam session

Stockholm, Sweden, c. February 1946

Reg Arnold, *tp*; Bob Henders, *tb*; Stan Hasselgard, *cl*; Ken Thorne, *p*; Vic Lewis, *g*; Simon Brehm, *b*; Harry Singer, *d*.

JAZZ ME BLUES	Harlequin HQ 3012

Vic Lewis and his orchestra

Private recordings, Star Sound Studios, Saturday, 23 November 1946

Reg Arnold, *tp*; Bunny Layzell, *tp*; Ken Summerville, *tp*; Fred Mercer, *tb*; Alfie Reece, *tb*; Ruth Harrison, *tb*; Ronnie Chamberlain, *cl, as, ss*; Peter Howe, *cl, as*; Jimmy Skidmore, *ts*; Charles Granville, *cl, ts*; Frank Holmes, *cl, as, bs*; Ken Thorne, *p, arr*; John Quest, *b*; Reg Swain, *d*; Helen Mack, *vcl*; Vic Lewis, *tb, dir*.

LAURA (Blue champagne theme)	Harlequin HQ 3013

Vic Lewis and his orchestra

Private recordings, Star Sound Studios, Tuesday, 3 December 1946

Reg Arnold, *tp*; Jack Parker, *tp*; Ken Summerville, *tp*; Ed Sweeney, *tb*; Alfie Reece, *tb*; Ruth Harrison, *tb*; Ronnie Chamberlain, *cl, as, ss*; Peter Howe, *cl, as, arr*; Jimmy Skidmore, *ts*; Charles Granville, *cl, ts*; Frank Holmes, *cl, as, bs*; Ken Thorne, *p, arr*; Al Ferdman, *g*; John Quest, *b*; Reg Swain, *d*; Helen Mack, *vcl*; Vic Lewis, *tb, dir*.

IN LOVE IN VAIN -*v* HM	Harlequin HQ 3013

Vic Lewis and his orchestra

Private recordings, Star Sound Studios, Friday, 6 December 1946

Ken Summerville, *arr*; Vic Lewis, *vcl*.

WELL GET IT	Harlequin HQ 3013

Vic Lewis and his orchestra

Overseas Radio Broadcasting Service, Tuesday, 17 December 1946

Peter Howe, *arr*.

BLUE CHAMPAGNE	
ALL REET -*ts* JS, *tp* RA, *tb* AR	DJM SPECB 103
IF I LOVE AGAIN -*a* KT, *tp* RA	DJM SPECB 103
I LIKE TO RIFF -*v* VL, *tp* RA	DJM SPECB 103
STRUT MISS LIZZIE (Jazzmen only)	
BLUE CHAMPAGNE	
APPLE HONEY -*a* PH, *ts* JS, *tb* VL, *c* I RC, *ts* CG, *tp* RA	DJM SPECB 103
PRELUDE TO A FRIEND -*a* KS, *tp* KS	
ROUND ABOUT EIGHT -(RC, KT, RS only)	DJM SPECB 103
A GOOD MAN IS HARD TO FIND -*v* VL	
WELL GET IT	
BLUE CHAMPAGNE/IT MIGHT AS WELL BE SWING -*a* KS	

Vic Lewis and his orchestra

30 January 1947

MAKING WHOOPEE	Harlequin HQ 3013

YOU'RE THE CAUSE OF IT ALL	Harlequin HQ 3013
IF I'M LUCKY	Harlequin HQ 3013
MOONLIGHT SERENADE	Harlequin HQ 3013

Vic Lewis and his orchestra
Saturday, 1 March 1947
Reg Arnold, *tp*; Jack Parker, *tp*; Johnny Shakespeare, *tp*; Alfie Reece, *tb*; Ed Sweeney, *tb*; Ruth Harrison, *tb*; Neal Saunders, *frh*; Laurie Saunders, *fl*; Moss Kaye, *oboe*; Ronnie Chamberlain, *cl, as*; Peter Howe, *cl, as*; Jimmy Skidmore, *ts*; Charles Granville, *ts*; Jerry Alvarez, *bs*; Frank Horrox, *p*; Al Ferdman, *g*; John Quest, *b*; Norman Burns, *d*; Frank Holmes, *vcl*; Helen Mack, *vcl*; Ken Thorne, *arr*; Vic Lewis, *dir*.

I CAN'T GET YOU OUT OF MY MIND -*v* FH, *a* KT	Vic Lewis Society DR 1347

Frank Holmes, *bs*, replaces Jerry Alvarez.

SOMEWHERE IN THE NIGHT -*v* HM, *a* KT	Vic Lewis Society DR 1347

Vic Lewis and his orchestra
Overseas Radio Broadcasting Service broadcast, Friday (morning), 7 March 1947
Reg Arnold, *tp*; Jack Parker, *tp*; Johnny Shakespeare, *tp*; Alfie Reece, *tb*; Ed Sweeney, *tb*; Ruth Harrison, *tb*; Ronnie Chamberlain, *cl, as, vcl*; Peter Howe, *cl, as, arr*; Jimmy Skidmore, *ts*; Charles Granville, *ts, vcl*; Frank Holmes, *bs, vcl*; Frank Horrox, *p*; Al Ferdman, *g*; John Quest, *b*; Reg Swain, *d*; Helen Mack, *vcl*; Ken Thorne, *arr*; Ken Summerville, *arr*; Vic Lewis, *tb, vcl, dir*.

SMILES	Harlequin HQ 3013

Vic Lewis and his jazzmen
Sunday, 23 March 1947
Reg Arnold, *tp*; Laddie Busby, *tb*; Ronnie Chamberlain, *cl, as*; Jimmy Skidmore, *ts*; Frank Holmes, *bs*; Ken Thorne, *p*; Al Ferdman, *g*; John Quest, *b*; Peter Coleman, *d*; Vic Lewis, *dir*.

AT THE JAZZ BAND BALL	Vic Lewis Society DR 1348, Esquire 10-022
PENNIES FROM HEAVEN	Vic Lewis Society DR 1348, Esquire 10-022

Vic Lewis and his orchestra
Monday, 23 June 1947
Johnny Shakespeare, *tp*; Bunny Layzell, *tp*; Vernon Thompson, *tp*; Fred Mercer, *tb*; Ed Sweeney, *tb*; Ruth Harrison, *tb*; Ronnie Chamberlain, *cl, as, ss*; Peter Howe, *cl, as*; Jimmy Skidmore, *ts*; Charles Granville, *ts, vcl*; Frank Holmes, *bs, vcl*; Ken Thorne, *p, arr*; Al Ferdman, *g*; John Quest, *b*; Peter Coleman, *d*; Vic Lewis, *vcl, dir*.

DARKTOWN POKER CLUB -*v* VL	Vic Lewis Society DR 1349
FOR YOU A BONE -*a* KT, *as* RC	Vic Lewis Society DR 1349, Esquire 10-021, Big Band International LP 2701
EINDAYZ -*a* KT, *ts* JS	Vic Lewis Society DR 1350, Esquire 10-021, Big Band International LP 2701
SUMMERTIME -*a* KT, *ss* RC	Vic Lewis Society DR 1350, Esquire 10-092, DJM SPECB 103

Vic Lewis and his orchestra
27 June 1947

RED TOP	Harlequin HQ 3013

Vic Lewis and his orchestra
Friday, 24 November 1947
Johnny Shakespeare, *tp*; Bunny Layzell, *tp*; Vernon Thompson, *tp*; Fred Mercer, *tb*; Ed Sweeney, *tb*; Jimmy Wilson, *tb*; Ronnie Chamberlain, *cl, as, ss*; Peter Howe, *cl, as*; Jimmy Skidmore, *ts*; Derek Knight, *ts*; Bill Collins, *bs*; Ken Thorne, *p, arr*; Al Ferdman, *g*; John Quest, *b*; Peter Coleman, *d*; Vic Lewis, *vcl, dir*.

LAURA -*a* KT, *as* RC	Parlophone R 3083, Big Band International LP 2701	CE12093
WHEN YOUR LOVER HAS GONE -*a* KT, *tb* JW	Parlophone R 3083, Big Band International LP 2701	CE 12094
COME BACK TO SORRENTO -*a* KT, *ts* JS	Parlophone R 3097, DJM SPECB 103	CE 12095
ARTISTRY IN PERCUSSION -*d* PC, *as* PH, *tb* JW	Parlophone R 3097, DJM SPECB 103	CE 12096-1

Vic Lewis and his orchestra

Monday (daytime), 23 February 1948

Johnny Shakespeare, *tp*; Bunny Layzell, *tp*; Vernon Thompson, *tp*; Billy Riddick, *tp*; Fred Mercer, *tb*; Ed Sweeney, *tb*; Jimmy Wilson, *tb*; Ronnie Chamberlain, *cl, as, ss*; Peter Howe, *cl, as*; Jimmy Walker, *ts*; Ken Beckett, *ts*; Bill Collins, *bs*; Ken Thorne, *p, arr*; Al Ferdman, *g*; John Quest, *b*; Peter Coleman, *d*; Vic Lewis, *dir*.

TOO FAT POLKA -*v* VL, *a* KT	CE12171 -2	Parlophone R 3101
THEY DIDN'T BELIEVE ME -*a* KT, *tp* JS	CE12172 -1	Parlophone R 3101, DJM SPECB 103
INDIAN SUMMER -*a* KT, *ss* RC	CE 12173	Big Band International LP 2701
BODY AND SOUL -*a* KT, *ts* JW	CE 12174	Big Band International LP 2701

Vic Lewis and his orchestra

Friday, 26 November 1948

Johnny Shakespeare, *tp*; Bunny Layzell, *tp*; Hank Shaw, *tp*; Harold Luff, *tp*; Don Lang, *tb*; Roy Bassett, *tb*; Jimmy Wilson, *tb*; Ronnie Chamberlain, *cl, as, ss*; Peter Howe, *cl, as*; Kathy Stobart, *ts, vcl*; Ken Beckett, *ts*; Bill Collins, *bs*; Dill Jones, *p*; Al Ferdman, *g*; John Quest, *b*; Peter Coleman, *d*; Lynda Russell, *vcl*; The Keynotes, vocal group; Ken Thorne, *arr*; Edwin Holland, *arr*; Vic Lewis, *vcl, arr*.

STARDUST	Harlequin HQ 3013
THE FOLKS WHO LIVE ON THE HILL -*a* KT, *as* RC	DJM SPECB 103

Vic Lewis and his orchestra

Friday, 3 December 1948

BODY AND SOUL	Harlequin HQ 3013

Vic Lewis and his orchestra

Film soundtrack, 'Vengeance Is Mine', early December 1948

Johnny Shakespeare, *tp*; Bunny Layzell, *tp*; Hank Shaw, *tp*; Harold Luff, *tp*; Don Lang, *tb*; Roy Bassett, *tb*; Jimmy Wilson, *tb*; Ronnie Chamberlain, *cl, as, ss*; Peter Howe, *cl, as*; Kathy Stobart, *ts*; Ken Beckett, *ts*; Bill Collins, *bs*; Dill Jones, *p*; Al Ferdman, *g*; John Quest, *b*; Peter Coleman, *d*; plus woodwinds and percussion; Vic Lewis, *dir*.

VENGEANCE IS MINE part 1	DJM SPECB 103
VENGEANCE IS MINE part 2	DJM SPECB 103

Vic Lewis and his orchestra

Tuesday, 25 January 1949

Johnny Shakespeare, *tp*; Bunny Layzell, *t*; Hank Shaw, *tp*; Harold Luff, *tp*; Don Lang, *tb*; Stan Smith, *tb*; Jack Waters, *tb*; Ronnie Chamberlain, *cl, as, ss*; Peter Howe, *cl, as, ss?*; Vince Bovil, *ts*; Kathy Stobart, *ts*; Bill Collins, *bs*; Dill Jones, *p*; Al Ferdman, *g*; Jack Honeyman, *b*; Peter Coleman, *d*; unknown perc; Ken Thorne, *arr*; Vic Lewis, *dir*.

WEST INDIAN RITUAL -*a* KT, *tb* DL	CE 12500 -1	Parlophone R 3183, Big Band International LP 2701
SUNDAY GIRL -*a* KT, *as* RC, *tb* DL	CE 12501 -1	Parlophone R 3183, PMC 7121, Big Band International LP 2701
HIGH ON A WINDY HILL -*a* KT, *ss* RC	CE 12502-1	Parlophone R 3208, Big Band International LP 2701
NO ORCHIDS -*a* KT, *ts* KS, *cl* RC	CE 12503 -1	Parlophone R 3208, Big Band International LP 2701

Vic Lewis and his orchestra

Paris Jazz Festival, France, Sunday, 8 May 1949
Micky Meene, *tp*; Johnny Oldfield, *tp*; Hank Shaw, *tp*; Harold Luff, *tp*; Don Lang, *tb*; Stan Smith, *tb*; Jack Waters, *tb*; Ronnie Chamberlain, *cl, as, ss*; Peter Howe, *cl, as, ss*; Vince Bovil, *ts*; Kathy Stobart, *ts, vcl*; Bill Collins, *bs*; Dill Jones, *p*; Al Ferdman, *g*; Jack Honeyman, *b*; Peter Coleman, *d*; Vic Lewis, *arr*.

EL SINO	Harlequin HQ 3013

Vic Lewis and his orchestra

Concert, Garrison Theatre, Hamburg, Germany, June 1949

ELEGY FOR ALTO -*a* PR, *as* RC	DJM SPECB 103

Vic Lewis and his orchestra

The following titles are probably from broadcasts from September 1949

SAFRANSKI -*a* PR	
YOU WAS -*v* KS, VL, *a* KT	DJM SPECB 103
INSPIRATION -*a* KT, *ts* KS	DJM SPECB 103
HARLEM HOLIDAY -*a* PR, *tp*?, *ts* KS, *tb* DL, *as* RC	Big Band International LP 2701
HEIR TO A CHINESE MAIDEN -*a* KT, *tb* DL	Big Band International LP 2701

Vic Lewis and his modern concert orchestra

Tuesday, 31 January 1950
Micky Meene, *tp*; Harry Finch, *tp*; Paul Berman, *tp*; Harold Luff, *tp*; Dennis Shirley, *tp*; Don Lang, *tb*; Stan Smith, *tb*; Tony Russell, *tb*; Eddie Harvey, *tb*; Johnny Keating, *tb*; Ronnie Chamberlain, *cl, as, ss*; Peter Howe, *cl, as, ss*; Vince Bovil, *ts*; Bob Efford, *ts*; Bill Collins, *bs*; Arthur Greenslade, *p*; Alan McDonald, *b*; Peter Coleman, *d*; Ken Thorne, *arr*; Pete Rugolo, *arr*; Vic Lewis, *dir*.

HAMMERSMITH RIFF -*a* PR, *as* RC, *tb* DL, *ts* BE	CE 12844 –1	Parlophone R 3273, DJM SPECB 103, Big Band International LP 2701
PEPPERPOT -*a* PR, *as* RC	CE 12845 –1	Parlophone R 3283, DJM SPECB 103
THE MAN I LOVE -*a* KT, *as* RC, *tb* DL, *tp* HL	CE 12846 –1	Parlophone R 3273, DJM SPECB 103, Big Band International LP 2701
MUSIC FOR MODERNS -*a* KT, *tb* DL, *as* RC	CE 12847 –1	Parlophone R 3283, DJM SPECB 103

Vic Lewis and his modern concert orchestra

BBC Light Programme broadcast, Monday, 16 February 1950

WHERE ARE YOU -*a* KT, *as* RC	DJM SPECB 103

Vic Lewis and his modern concert orchestra

Monday, 24 April 1950
Add Ken Goldie, *tb*.

I'LL REMEMBER APRIL -*v* JJ, *a* PR	CE12904	Parlophone rejected
DESIGN FOR BRASS -*a* PR, *as* RC, *tb* JK, *ts* BE, *tp* HL	CE 12905	Parlophone R 3289, DJM SPECB 103
THEME FOR ALTO -*a* PR, *as* RC	CE12906	Parlophone R 3289, DJM SPECB 103
THEME FOR TROMBONE -*a* PR, *tb* JK	CE 12907	Parlophone R 3299, Big Band Int. LP 2701

Vic Lewis and his modern concert orchestra

Friday, 26 May 1950

OVER THE RAINBOW -*v* JJ, *a* PR, *tb* DL	CE 12953	Parlophone R 3299
SERENADE IN BLUE -*a* KT, *as* RC	CE 12954	Parlophone R 3315, Big Band Int. LP 2701
A HUNDRED YEARS FROM TODAY -*v* VL, *a* PR, *tp* DS	CE12955	DJM SPECB 103
LOVE FOR SALE -*a* PR, *tb* DL	CE12956	Parlophone R 3315, Big Band Int. LP 2701

Vic Lewis and his orchestra
Friday, 18 August 1950

THREE BOP	Harlequin HQ 3013

Vic Lewis and his orchestra
Tuesday, 27 February 1951

YOU GO TO MY HEAD -*v* MW, *a* JK	Esquire 5-029
DEED I DO -*v* MW, *a* JK, *as* RC	Esquire 5-029
JUST ONE OF THOSE THINGS -*v* MW, *a* JK	Esquire 5-018
RHAPSODY IN BLUE part 1 -*a* JK, *cl* PH	Esquire 5-019
RHAPSODY IN BLUE part 2 -*a* JK, *cl* PH	Esquire 5-019
THINKING OF YOU -*a* JK, *tp* SR, *ts* RS	Esquire 5-018, Big Band International LP 2701
SOLITARE -*a* JK, *tb* JK	Esquire 10-124, Discovery 1752, Big Band International LP 2701,
LEMON DROP -*v* VL, MW, *a* SR, *ts* RS, *tp* DU, *as* RC	Esquire 10-124
LEMON DROP (alternate take) -*v* VL, MW, *a* SR, *ts* RS, *tp* DU, *as* RC	Esquire LP 20-2011

Vic Lewis and his orchestra
Monday, 7 May 1951
Bert Courtley, *tp*; Stan Reynolds, *tp*; Ronnie Simmonds, *tp*; Terry Lewis, *tp*; Ken Goldie, *tb*; Johnny Keating, *tb*, *arr*; Ronnie Chamberlain, *cl*, *as*, *ss*; Derek Humble, *cl*, *as*; Peter Warner, *ts*; Kathy Stobart, *ts*, *vcl*; Jimmy Simmonds, *bs*; Arthur Greenslade, *p*; Pete Blannin, *b*; Peter Coleman, *d*; Marion Williams, *vcl*; Edwin Holland, *arr*; Pete Rugolo, *arr*; Al Cohn, *arr*; Vic Lewis, *vcl*, *dir*.

VIC'S RIFF -*a* PR, mute *tp* BC, *tb* JK, *as* DH, *ts* KS	Esquire 10-134, Big Band International LP 2701
EVERYWHERE -*a* JK, *tb* JK	Esquire 10-144,
BE MY LOVE -*a* JK, *as* RC, *ss* RC, *tp* SR	Esquire 15-024, Big Band International LP 2701
THE APPLE -*a* AC, *tp* BC, *ts* KS	Esquire 10-144, Discovery 1752, LP 2001
	Big Band International LP 2701
FESTIVAL RIFF -*a* EH, *tp* BC	Esquire 10-134, Big Band International LP 2701
THE MOON WAS YELLOW -*a* JK, *ss* RC	Esquire 10-174, Big Band International LP 2701
A FOGGY DAY -*a* JK, *cl* DH	Esquire 10-174, Big Band International LP 2701

Omit brass except Johnny Keating, *tb*
TEA FOR TWO *v* MW, *a* JK, *as* RC, *cl* DH, *ts* KS
Esquire 15-024

Vic Lewis and his orchestra
97th General Hospital USAF *broadcast,* AFN *Frankfurt, Germany, Wednesday, 11 September 1951*
add Vic Lewis, *tb*;

THE CARIOCA -*a* JK, *tb* JK, *ts* KS, *cl* DH, *tb* VL	Big Band International LP 2701

Vic Lewis and his new music
Wednesday, 26 March 1952
Johnny Dankworth, *arr*

WHY DO I LOVE YOU -*a* DA	Esquire 10-222
JD TO VL -*a* JD	Esquire 10-232
STREET SCENE -*a* DA	Esquire 10-222
HERU -*a* DA	Esquire 10-232

Vic Lewis and his orchestra

Wednesday, 13 January 1954
Les Condon, *tp*; Ronnie Baker, *tp*; Dave Loban, *tp*; Colin Wright, *tp*; Laurie Franklin, *tb*; Jack Botterill, *tb*; Johnny Watson, *tb*; Laddie Busby, *tb*; Ronnie Chamberlain, *cl, as, ss*; Bernard Allen, *as*; Les Wigfield, *ts*; Tubby Hayes, *ts, bs*; Brian Rodgerson, *bs*; Don Riddle, *p*; Dave Willis, *b*; Kenny Hollick, *d*; Johnny Keating, *arr*; Gerry Mulligan, *arr*; Ken Thorne, *arr*; Dave Lindup, *arr*; Bill Oliver, *arr*; Vic Lewis, *dir*.

WALKIN' SHOES -*a* GM, *tb* LB, *ts* TH, *as* RC, *tp* LC	Decca LF 1157, London LB 980, Mole 9
SEXTET -*a* JK, *tb* LB, *as* RC, *ts* TH, *tp* LC	Decca LF 1157, London LB 980, Mole 9

Vic Lewis and his orchestra

Thursday, 14 January 1954

LINE FOR LYONS -*a* JK, *tb* JW, *ts* LW, *as* RC, *tp* LC	Decca LF 1157, London LB 980, Mole 9
NIGHTS AT THE TURNTABLE -*a* JK, *ts* RH, *tb* JW	Decca LF 1157, London LB 980, Mole 9
BWEEBIDA BOBBIDA -*a* GM, *tp* CW, *as* RC, *ts* TH	Decca LF 1157, London LB 980, Mole 9
LIMELIGHT -*a* GM, *as* RC, *ts* TH, *tb* LB, *tp* LC	Decca LF 1157, London LB 980, Mole 9

Vic Lewis and his orchestra

Wednesday, 20 January 1954

BARK FOR BARKSDALE -*a* JK, *bs* TH	Decca F 10260, 45 F 10260, LF 1157, London LF 980, DJM SPECB 103, Mole 9
WESTWOOD WALK -*a* JK, *as* RC, *ts* TH, *tp* LC	Decca LF 1157, London LF 980, Mole 9

add Stan Roderick, *tp*; George Chisholm, *tb*

HAPPY HORNBLOWERS -*a* BO, *mtp* LC	Decca F 10260, 45 F 10260, DJM SPECB 103

Vic Lewis and his orchestra

Concert, City Hall, Sheffield, Saturday, 23 January 1954
Dave Power, *tp*; Ronnie Baker, *tp*; Dave Loban, *tp*; Colin Wright, *tp*; Laurie Franklin, *tb*; Jack Botterill, *tb*; Johnny Watson, *tb*; Alec Gould, *tb, arr*; Ronnie Chamberlain, *cl, as, ss*; Bernard Allen, *as*; Les Wigfield, *ts*; Tubby Hayes, *ts, bs*; Brian Rodgerson, *bs*; Don Riddle, *p*; Dave Willis, *b*; Kenny Hollick, *d*; Roy Garnett, *vcl*; Johnny Keating, *arr*; Gerry Mulligan, *arr*; Ken Thorne, *arr*; Bill Russo, *arr*; Shorty Rogers, *arr*; Ray Wetzel, *arr*; Pete Rugolo, *arr*; Bill Holman, *arr*; Gene Roland, *arr*; Dave Lindup, *arr*; Vic Lewis, *dir*.

BILL'S BLUES -*a* BR, *tp* DP, *ts* TH	Hep 20
HARLEM NOCTURNE -*a* BR, *tb* JB	Hep 20, Big Band International LP 2705
JOLLY ROGERS -*a* SR, *tp* DP, *as* RC	Hep 20
MOONLIGHT IN VERMONT -*a* KT, *tb* JW, *as* RC	Hep 20
TOO MARVELLOUS FOR WORDS (*ts* TH + rhythm only)	Hep 20
THEME FOR FOUR VALUES -*a* BR, *tb* JW	Big Band International LP 2705
YOU'D BE SO NICE TO COME HOME TO -*a* BR	Harlequin 1014
BWEEBIDA BOBBIDA -*a* GM, *tp* DP, *as* RC, *ts* TH	Hep 20, Big Band International LP 2705
PEANUT VENDOR -*a* PR, *tb* JW, *ts* TH	Hep 20
FEARLESS FOSDIKE -*a* BJ, *tp* RB, *as* RC, *tb* LF	Hep 20, Big Band International LP 2705
SEXTETTE -*a* JK, *tb* JB, *as* RC, *ts* TH, *tp* CW	Hep 20
JUMP FOR JOE -*a* GR, *as* RC	Hep 20
THE CREEP -*a* JK, *as* RC, *ts* TH	Hep 20

SEVEN ELEVEN (incomplete)	Unissued
(-*tp* CW, *as* RC, *ts* LW + rhythm only)	
SEVEN ELEVEN (complete)	Unissued
(-*tp* CW, *as* RC, *ts* LW + rhythm only)	
WALKIN' SHOES -*a* GM, *as* RC, *ts* TH, *tb* JW, *tp* CW	Hep 20
LIMELIGHT -*a* GM, *as* RC, *ts* TH, *tb* JW, *tp* DP	Hep 20
EBB TIDE -*v* DR, *a* KT	Unissued
CARNAVALITO	Unissued
BARK FOR BARKSDALE -*a* JK, *ts* TH	Hep 20
INTERMISSION RIFF -*a* RW, *ts* LW, TH, *tp* CW, *tb* JW, *as* BA, RC	Hep 20
GOD SAVE THE QUEEN -*a* DL	Unissued

Note: Hep 20 gives 29 January 1954, but band played at Radcliff on this date. Correct date is as shown above.

Vic Lewis and his orchestra

BBC Light Programme broadcast, Tuesday, 9 November 1954

LATER GEORGE -*a* RM, *ts* BG, *tp* JB, *as* RC	Big Band International LP 2701

Vic Lewis and his orchestra

Thursday, 18 November 1954

Johnny Brown, *tp*; Ronnie Baker, *tp*; Dave Loban, *tp*; Trevor Lannigan, *tp*; Johnny Watson, *tb*; Rusty Hurran, *tb*, *vcl*; Alec Gould, *tb*; Johnny Keating, *tb*, *arr*; Ronnie Chamberlain, *cl*, *as*, *ss*; Bernard Allen, *as*; Brian Gray, *ts*; Howard Morgan, *ts*; Brian Rodgerson, *bs*; Red Mitchell, *p*; Stan Wasser, *b*; Andy White, *d*; Johnny Keating, *arr*; Gerry Mulligan, *arr*; Bill Holman, *arr*; Shorty Rogers, *arr*; Vic Lewis, *dir*.

BEGIN THE BEGUINE -*a* GM, *as* RC, *tp* RB	Esquire 10-421, EP33
THE OPENER -*a* BH, *tb* AG, *as* RC, *tp* RB	Esquire 10-421, EP 33
SHORT STOP -*a* SR, *as* RC, *ts* BG, *tp* JB	Esquire 10-422, EP 33
ARUAL -*a* JK, *ts* BG, *tp* JB, *as* RC	Esquire 10-422, EP 33

Vic Lewis and his orchestra

Concert, Royal Festival Hall, Sunday, 9 January 1955

Johnny Brown, *tp*; Ronnie Baker, *tp*; Dave Loban, *tp*; Trevor Lannigan, *tp*; Johnny Watson, *tb*; Andy Wilson, *tb*; Rusty Hurran, *tb*, *vcl*; Alec Gould, *tb*, *arr*; Ronnie Chamberlain, *cl*, *as*, *ss*; Bernard Allen, *as*; Brian Gray, *ts*; Howard Morgan, *ts*; Brian Rodgerson, *bs*; Red Mitchell, *p*; Len Edwards, *b*; Andy White, *d*; Johnny Keating, *arr*; Gerry Mulligan, *arr*; Bill Oliver, *arr*; Ken Thorne, *arr*; Dave Lindup, *arr*; Bill Russo, *arr*; Bill Holman, *arr*; Shorty Rogers, *arr*; Don Riddle, *arr*; Pete Rugolo, *arr*; Vic Lewis, *dir*.

SWINGHOUSE -*a* GM, *tb* AG, *as* RC, *ts* BG, *tp* JB	Decca LF 1216, Mole 9
CHINO -*a* SR, *tp* JB, *tb* AG, *tp* JB	Decca LF 1216, Mole 9
STAR EYES -*a* BH, *tp* JB, *tb* AG	Decca LF 1216, Mole 9
COUP DE GRAAS -*a* SR, *tb* AG, *ts* BG	Mole 9
DUO -*a* AG, *as* RC, *tp* JB	Decca LF 1216, Mole 9
BARK FOR BARKSDALE -*a* JK, *d* AW	Decca LF 1216
DANCING IN THE DARK -*a* GM, *ts* BG, *tp* JB	Decca LF 1216, Mole 9
SHORT STOP -*a* SR, *as* RC, *tp* JB, *ts* BG	Mole 9
PEANUT VENDOR -*a* PR, *tb* JW, *as* RC, *ts* BG	Decca LF 1216, Mole 9

Vic Lewis and his orchestra

Wednesday, 2 February 1955

Johnny Brown, *tp*; Ronnie Baker, *tp*; Dave Loban, *tp*; Trevor Lannigan, *tp*; Gordon Sardella, *tp*; Johnny Watson, *tb*; Ken Goldie, *tb*; Rusty Hurran, *tb*; Alec Gould, *tb*; Laddie Busby, *tb*; Ronnie Chamberlain, *as*; Bernard Allen, *as*; Brian Gray, *ts*; Howard Morgan, *ts*; Brian Rodgerson, *bs*; Red Mitchell, *p*, *arr*; Len Edwards, *b*; Andy White, *d*; Bill Oliver, *arr*; Vic Lewis, *dir*.

DON'T SAY GOODBYE -*a* RM, *mtp* TL	Philips PB 411
BARWICK GREEN -*a* BO	Philips PB 411
SLOWLY BUT SURELY -*a* BO	Philips PB 414
CHERRY RIPE -*a* BO	Philips PB 414

Vic Lewis and his orchestra

Tuesday, 3 May 1955
Ian Hamier, *tp*; Carl Shafto, *tp*; Dave Loban, *tp*; Gordon Sardella, *tp*; Johnny Watson, *tb*; Ken Goldie, *tb*; Kevin Neal, *tb*; Alec Gould, *tb*; Ronnie Chamberlain, *as*; Roy East, *as*; Art Ellefson, *ts*; Howard Morgan, *ts*; Brian Rodgerson, *bs*; Red Mitchell, *p*; Ken Williams, *b*; Andy White, *d*; Bill Oliver, *arr*; Shorty Rogers, *arr*; Vic Lewis, *vcl, dir*.

THE ASH GROVE -*a* BO, *tb* JW, AG, *as* RE	Philips PB 466, DJM SPECB 103
STRAWBERRY FAIR -*a* BO, *tp* GS, *ts* AE	Philips PB 466, DJM SPECB 103
WALK DON'T RUN -*a* SR, *as* RE, *tp* GS, *tb* AG, *as* RC, *ts* AE	Philips PB 503, DJM SPECB 103
SCRAMBLE -*a* SR, *as* RC, *tp* IH, *ts* AE, *tb* AG	Philips PB 503, DJM SPECB 103

Johnnie Ray with Vic Lewis and his orchestra

Tuesday, 3 May 1955
add 14 strings, Johnnie Ray, *vcl*.

MY LOVE FOR YOU -*v* JR, *a* BO	Philips PB 463

omit strings

TAKING A CHANCE ON LOVE -*v* JR	Philips PB 463

Vic Lewis and his orchestra

Wednesday, 26 September 1956

INTERMISSION ROCK -*a* AG, *tp* DM, *as* CB	Decca FJ 10803, 45 FJ 10803, DJM SPECB 103
INTERMISSION ROCK (extended version)	unissued
NATAL -*a* AG, *tp* DM	Decca FJ 10803, 45 FJ 10803, DJM SPECB 103
NATAL (extended version)	unissued

Vic Lewis and his orchestra

Concert, University of Connecticut, USA, Wednesday, 12 March 1958
Dickie McPherson, *tp*; Joe McIntyre, *tp*; Al Spooner, *tp*; Kenny Wheeler, *tp, arr*; Alec Gould, *tb, arr*; Colin Bradfield, *as*; Ronnie Baker, *as*; Bobby Wellins, *ts*; Duncan Lamont, *ts*; Brian Rodgerson, *bs*; Gerry Butler, *p, arr*; Bill Stark, *b*; Bobby Orr, *d*; Irma Logan, *vcl*; Ronnie Roulier, *arr*, Bill Holman, *arr*; Art Ellefson, *arr*; Johnny Richards, *arr*; Gerry Mulligan, *arr*; Buddy Johnson, *arr*; Johnny Keating, *arr*; Alan Lowe, *arr*; Vic Lewis, *p, vcl, arr, dir*.

THAT'S LOVE -*a* AG, *as* CB	DJM SPECB 103
OVER THE RAINBOW -*a* KW, *tp* KW	DJM SPECB 103
EL CONGO VALIENTE -*a* JR, *as* RB?, *tp* KW	DJM SPECB 103

One world jazz

NYC, Tuesday, 19 May 1959
Clark Terry, *tp*; J. J. Johnson, *tb*; Ben Webster, *ts*; Hank Jones, *p*; Kenny Burrell, *g*; George Duvivier, *b*; Jo Jones, *d*.
London, Monday, 22 June 1959
George Chisholm, *tb*; Roy East, *as*; Ronnie Ross, *bs*; Vic Lewis, *dir*.
Stockholm, Sweden, Tuesday, 30 June 1959
Ake Persson, *tb*.
Paris, France, Friday, 3 July 1959
Roger Guerin, *tp*; Bob Garcia, *ts*; Martial Solal, *p*; Stéphane Grappelli, *vln*.

MISTY
INTERNATIONAL BLUES
COTTON TAIL
NUAGES
IN A MELLOWTONE
BIG BEN BLUES

All tracks on: Columbia WL 162, WS 314, Philips BBL 7361, B 07568 L, CBS 1500

Vic Lewis and his jazz group

Wednesday, 24 June 1959
Eddie Blair, *tp*; Les Condon, *tp*; George Chisholm, *tb*; Roy East, *as*; Ronnie Scott, *ts*; Ronnie Ross, *bs*;

Alan Branscombe, *p*; Bill Sutcliffe, *b*; Dave Pearson, *d*; Alec Gould, *arr*; John Dankworth, *arr*; Vic Lewis, *dir*.

I NEVER KNEW A LOVE LIKE THIS -*a* JD	Concept VL 5
SALT PEANUTS	Concept VL 5
MOUNT BAYOU -*a* AG	Concept VL 5
LITTLE GIRL -*a* AG	Concept VL 5
PENSYLVANIA TURNPIKE -*a* AG, *tp* EB	Concept VL 5
STANHOPE PLACE -*a* AG	Concept VL 5

Vic Lewis and his all stars

June 1959

Dickie McPherson, *tp*; Jimmy Deuchar, *tp*; Leon Calvert, *tp*; Gordon Turnbull, *tp*; Keith Christie, *tb*; Roy East, *as*; Vic Ash, *cl, ts*; Art Ellefson, *ts*; Ronnie Ross, *bs*; Terry Shannon, *p*; Arthur Watts, *b*; Allan Ganley, *d*; Alec Gould, *arr*; Tony Crombie, *arr*; Vic Lewis, *dir*.

THE BEAULIEU SUITE:	
BEAULIEU BLUES -*a* TC, *tp* JD, LC, *ts* AE, VA	Ember CJS 807, SE 8018
LADY BELINDA -*a* TC	Ember CJS 807, SE 8018
MOTOR MUSEUM -*a* TC, *ts* AE, *tp* JD, LC	Ember CJS 807, SE 8018
DOMUS -*a* TC	Ember CJS 807, SE 8018
MONTY -*a* TC, *tp* JD	Ember CJS 807, SE 8018

Vic Lewis and his all stars

June 1959

Kenny Wheeler, *tp*; replaces Gordon Turnbull.

SELECTIONS FROM THE SPRINBOK & AMERICAN SUITES:	Ember CJS 807, SE 8018
GOLD DUST -AG, *tp* KW	

Vic Lewis and his all stars

June 1959

Dickie McPherson, *tp*; Jimmy Deuchar, *tp*; Leon Calvert, *tp*; Gordon Turnbull, *tp*; Keith Christie, *tb*; Roy East, *as*; Vic Ash, *cl, ts*; Art Ellefson, *ts*; Ronnie Ross, *bs*; Terry Shannon, *p*; Arthur Watts, *b*; Allan Ganley, *d*; Alec Gould, *arr*; Vic Lewis, *dir*.

SELECTIONS FROM THE SPRINGBOK & AMERICAN SUITES:	
DOBBS FERRY -*a* AG, *tp* JD, *ts* VA	Ember CJS 807, SE 8018
THE JACARANDA TREE -*a* AG, *ts* VA	Ember CJS 807, SE 8018
BEAU KAI -*a* AG, *ts* AE, *tp* JD	Ember CJS 807, SE 8018
THE FORREST -*a* AG, *tp* JD, *ts* AE	Ember CJS 807, SE 8018

Vic Lewis and his orchestra

Concert, Bridgeport, Connecticut, USA, Sunday, 10 April 1960

Dickie McPherson, *tp*; Jimmy Deuchar, *tp, arr*; Leon Calvert, *tp*; Gordon Turnbull, *tp*; Keith Christie, *tb*; Roy East, *as, fl*; Vic Ash, *cl, ts*; Art Ellefson, *ts*; Ronnie Ross, *bs*; Terry Shannon, *p*; Ray Dempsey, *g*; Arthur Watts, *b*; Allan Ganley, *d*; Shelly Moore, *vcl*; Tony Crombie, *arr*; Vic Lewis, *vcl, dir*.

PORT OF SPAIN -*a* JD, *ts* AE, *tp* JD, *ts* VA, *tp* LF	DJM SPECB 103
LITTLE DARLING -*mtp* JD	DJM SPECB 103

Vic Lewis and his orchestra

Monday, 9 July 1962

Bert Ezzard, *tp*; Bert Courtley, *tp*; Eddie Blair, *tp*; Duncan Cambell, *tp*; Keith Christie, *tb*; Johnny Edwards, *tb*; Ken Goldie, *tb*; Ronnie Chamberlain, *as*; Johnny Scott, *as*; Bob Efford, *ts*; Henry McKenzie, *ts*; Ken Kiddier, *bs*; Derek Warne, *p*; Dave Goldberg, *g*; Johnny Hawksworth, *b*; Jack Parnell, *d*; Nelson Riddle, *arr*; Vic Lewis, *dir*.

BASIEC RIDDLE -*a* NR, *tp* EB, BC	DJM SPECB 103
THE BASS IS LOADED -*a* NR, *tp* BC, *tb* KC	
SAX BLUE -*a* NR, *as* RC	
TOWN TALK -*a* NR, *tp* EB	

All tracks on: Columbia SEG 8202, Big Band International LP 2701.

Vic Lewis and his bossa nova all stars

Los Angeles, Ca, USA, Friday, 18 January 1963
Jack Sheldon, *tp*; Shorty Rogers, *flh*, *arr*; Bud Shank, *ts*, *fl*; Bob Cooper, *ts*; Vic Feldman, *p*, vibes; Al Hendrickson, *g*; Don Bagley, *b*; Shelly Manne, *d*; Howard Lucraft, *arr*; Leonard Feather, *arr*; Vic Lewis, *dir*, *arr*.

BOSSA NOVA SCOTIA -*a* HL, *ts* BV	HMV CLP 1641, CSD 1492, POP 1127
RIO -*a* HL, *ts* BS	HMV CLP 1641, CSD 1492
TWO NOTE SAMBA -*a* SR, *ts* BC, BC	HMV CLP 1641, CSD 1492, DJM SPECB 103

add Laurindo Almeida, *g*

BOSSA NOVA BLUES -*a* LF, *ts* BC	HMV CLP 1641, CSD 1492

Vic Lewis and his bossa nova all stars

Friday, 8 February 1963
Jimmy Deuchar, *tp*, *mellophone*, *arr*; Shake Keane, *tp*, *flh*; Tubby Hayes, *ts*, *fl*, *arr*; Ronnie Scott, *ts*; Terry Shannon, *p*; Ray Dempsey, *g*; Freddy Logan, *b*; Kenny Clare, *d*; Johnny Keating, *arr*; Vic Lewis, *arr*.

VIC'S TUNE -*a* JK, *ts* RS	HMV CLP 1641, CSD 1492, POP 1127
RICARDO -*a* TH, *ts* TH	HMV CLP 1641, CSD 1492, DJM SPECB 103
DANIELLE -*a* JD, *ts* RS, TH	HMV CLP 1641, CSD 1492
LAST MINUTE BOSSA NOVA-*a* RS, *ts* RS	HMV CLP 1641, CSD 1492

Vic Lewis and his orchestra

28 April 1967
Stéphane Grappelli, solo *vln*; Tony Gilbert, *vln*; Brian Hill, *vln*; Dennis McConnell, *vln*; Alan Peters, *vln*; John Jezzard, *vln*; Laurie Lewis, *vln*; Jurgen Hess, *vln*; Bernard Harris, *vln*; Maurice Linden, *vln*; Ted Bryett, *vln*; George French, *vln*; Paul Harris, *viola*; Jack Fleetcroft, *viola*; Maurice Clayman, *viola*; Michael Freedman, *viola*; Jack Long, *cello*; Dennis Southard, *cello*; Charles Ford, *cello*; David Smith, *cello*; Jim Buck, *frh*; Alan Civil, *frh*; David Snell, *horn*; Laurie Holloway, *p*, *harpsichord*; Arthur Watts, *b*; John Honeyman, *b*; Stan Gorman, *perc*; John Blanchard, *perc*; Granville Jones, *leader*; Ken Thorne, *arr*; Vic Lewis, *cond*.

TWO FOR THE ROAD -*a* KT	CBS 2834, DJM SPECB 103
STEPPS -*a* KT	CBS 2834, Nems (s) 6-63561

The Vic Lewis orchestra

Monday, 17 June; Tuesday, 18 June; Wednesday, 19 June 1968
John Sharpe, *vln*; Granville Jones, *vln*; Charles McKeown, *vln*; Alan Peters, *vln*; Paul Sherman, *vln*; Laurie Lewis, *vln*; Jack Harris, *vln*; Leslie Maddox, *vln*; Norman Lederman, *vln*; David Bellman, *viola*; Henry Myerscough, *viola*; Brian Thomas, *viola*; Ray Patten, *viola*; Francis Gabarro, *cello*; Dennis Southard, *cello*; Charles Ford, *cello*; Peter Halling, *cello*; Alan Civil, *frh*; Nula Herbert, *horn*; Ian Black, *oboe*; Harold McNair, *fl*; Danny Moss, *ts*; Laurie Holloway, *p*, *harpsichord*; Alan Parker, *g*; Frank Clarke, *b*; John Honeyman, *b*; Tony Carr, *perc*; Alan Grahame, *perc*; Joan Brown, *solo voice*; Sidney Sax, *leader*; John Cameron, *arr*; Vic Lewis, *cond*.

SUNSHINE SUPERMAN	Nems 56-3712, Epic BM 26418
MELLOW YELLOW -*ts* DM	Nems 56-3712, Epic BM 26418
THERE IS A MOUNTAIN	Epic BM 26418
A BOY CALLED DONOVAN	Nems (s) 6-63561
POOR COW	Epic BM 26418
LELENIA	Epic BM 26418
THREE KINGFISHERS	Epic BM 26418
HURDY GURDY MAN	Epic BM 26418
JENNIFER JUNIPER	Epic BM 26418
LORD OF THE REEDY RIVER	Epic BM 26418
CATCH THE WIND	Epic BM 26418
YOUNG GIRL'S BLUES -*ts* DM	Epic BM 26418
A SUNNY DAY	Epic BM 26418
THE BOY WITH THE SAFFRON ROBE	Nems (s) 6-63561

The Vic Lewis orchestra

Thursday, 18 July 1968

Harold McNair, *fl*; Ian Black, *oboe*; John Sharpe, *vln*; Charles McKeown, *vln*; Paul Scherman, *vln*; Laurie Lewis, *vln*; Jack Harris, *vln*; Jack Mandel, *vln*; Norman Lederman, *vln*; Desmond Bradley, *vln*; Ray Mosley, *vln*; Dennis McConnell, *vln*; Eric Eaden, *vln*; David Bellman, *viola*; Henry Myerscough, *viola*; Michael Freedman, *viola*; Roy Patten, *viola*; Francis Gabarro, *cello*; Charles Ford, *cello*; Peter Halling, *cello*; Dennis Southard, *cello*; David Snell, *harp*; Laurie Holloway, *p, harpsichord*; Ernie Shear, *g*; Frank Clarke, *b*; Rodney Stewart, *b*; Tony Carr, *perc*; Tristan Fry, *perc*; Sidney Sax, *ldr*; Vic Lewis, *cond.*

DIANA	Nems (s) 6-63561

The Vic Lewis orchestra

Saturday, 16 November 1968

John Sharpe, *vln*; Ray Mosley, *vln*; Charles McKeown, *vln*; Alan Peters, *vln*; Paul Scherman, *vln*; Laurie Lewis, *vln*; Jack Harris, *vln*; Peter Benson, *vln*; Eric Bowie, *vln*; Dennis McConnell, *vln*; Len Dight, *vln*; John Harris, *viola*; Don Thompson, *viola*; Brian Thomas, *viola*; Roy Patten, *viola*; Michael Freedman, *viola*; Tom Lister, *viola*; Ian Jewel, *viola*; Max Gilbert, *viola*; Jack Long, *cello*; Dennis Southard, *cello*; Charles Ford, *cello*; David Smith, *cello*; Peter Willison, *cello*; John Burden, *frh*; Tryphena Patridge, *horn*; Ian Black, *oboe*; Harold McNair, *fl*; Ronnie Chamberlain, *as*; Danny Moss, *ts*; Ray Swinfield, *sax*; Alan Hawkshaw, *p, harpsichord*; Ernie Shear, *g*; Spike Heatley, *b*; John Honeyman, *b*; Tony Carr, *perc*; Tristan Fry, *prec*; Mike Sammes Singers, *vocal group*; Sidney Sax, *leader*; John Cameron, *arr*; Vic Lewis, *cond.*

GOODNIGHT -*v* MSS, *a* JC	Nems 56-3893, (s) 6-63723, DJM DJSL 030, CBS Sony SONY 60118
JULIA -*v* MSS, *a* JC	Nems 56-3893, (s) 6-63723, DJM DJSL 030, CBS Sony SONY 60118
LONG WHITE NIGHTS -*a* JC	Nems (s) 6-63561
ANDANTE -*a* JC	Nems (s) 6-63561
LOVE OF A COUNTRY GIRL -*a* JC	Nems (s) 6-63561

The Vic Lewis orchestra

Sunday, 8 December 1968

Alan Loveday, *vln*; Les Maddox, *vln*; Charles McKeown, *vln*; Jack Mandel; *vln*; Paul Scherman, *vln*; Laurie Lewis, *vln*; Jack Harris, *vln*; Peter Benson, *vln*; Eric Bowie, *vln*; Dennis McConnell, *vln*; Len Dight, *vln*; David Bellman, *viola*; Henry Myerscough, *viola*; John Meek, *viola*; Michael Freedman, *viola*; Jack Long, *cello*; Dennis Southard, *cello*; Charles Ford, *cello*; Peter Halling, *viola*; John Marshall, *tb*; Bobby Lamb, *tb*; Keith Christie, *tb*; Chris Pyne, *tb*; John Watson, *tb*; John Burden, *frh*; David Snell, *horn*; Ian Black, *oboe*; Harold McNair, *fl*; Danny Moss, *ts*; Ronnie Price, *p*; Dick Abel, *g*; Spike Heatley, *b*; John Honeyman, *b*; Tony Carr, *perc*; Alan Grahame, *prec*; Mike Sammes Singers, *vocal group*; Sidney Sax, *leader*; John Cameron, *arr*; Johnny Keating, *arr*; Vic Lewis, *cond.*

BLACKBIRD -*v* MSS, *a* JC	Nems 56-4057, (s) 6-63723, DJM DJSL 030, CBS Sony SONY 60118
I WILL -*v* MSS, *a* JC	Nems 56-4057, (s) 6-63723, DJM DJSL 030, CBS Sony SONY 60118
KLIN -*a* JC	Nems (s) 6-63561
PRELUDE -*a* JC	Nems (s) 6-63561

add Maynard Ferguson, *tp*

THE OTHER WOMAN -*a* JK	Nems (s) 6-63561, DJM SPECB 103

The Vic Lewis orchestra

Friday, 6 June 1969

Tony Fisher, *flh*; Les Condon, *flh*; Don Lusher, *tb*; Johnny Watson, *tb*; Andrew McGavin, *frh*; Jim Brown, *frh*; Jim Buck, *frh*; Douglas Moore, *frh*; Alfie Reece, *tu*; Harold McNair, *fl*; Bill Skeat, *fl*; Ian

Black, *oboe*; Danny Moss, *cl*; Ronnie Ross, *cl*; Bunny Gould, *bassoon*; Boris Rickleman, *cello*; Bram Martin, *cello*; Charles Ford, *cello*; Peter Halling, *cello*; David Snell, *horn*; Laurie Holloway, *p*; John Williams, *solo g*; Dick Abel, *g*; Danny Thompson, *b*; Tony Carr, *d*; Tristan Fry, *perc*; John Cameron, *arr*; Vic Lewis, *cond*.

> She's Leaving Home *-a* JC, *g* JW
> Norwegian Wood *-a* JC, *g* JW   DJM SPECB 103
> Fool on the Hill *-a* JC
> Yesterday *-a* JC

All tracks on: Nems (s) 6-63723, DJM DJSL 030, CBS Sony SONY 60118

The Vic Lewis orchestra

Thursday, 12 June 1969

Tony Fisher, *tp*; Les Condon, *tp*; Chris Pyne, *tb*; Johnny Watson, *tb*; Barry Castle, *frh*; Douglas Moore, *frh*; Norman Knight, *fl*; George Crozier, *fl*; Ian Black, *oboe*; Danny Moss, *cl*; Les Ormondroyd, *cl*; Joe Castaldini, *bassoon*; Eric Haden, *vln*; Michael Rennie, *vln*; Charles McKeown, *vln*; Laurie Clay, *vln*; Alan Peters, *vln*; Laurie Lewis, *vln*; Jack Harris, *vln*; Roy Davis, *vln*; Jim Archer, *vln*; Reg Cole, *vln*; Homy Kanga, *vln*; James Soutter, *vln*; Maurice Cybula, *vln*; John Davis, *vln*; Nat Conras, *vln*; Norman Lederman, *vln*; David Bellman, *viola*; Tom Lister, *viola*; John Meek, *vln*; Michael Freedman, *viola*; John Coulding, *viola*; Ben Thomas, *viola*; Francis Gabarro, *cello*; Peter Willison, *cello*; Robert Kik, *cello*; Dennis Southard, *cello*; David Snell, *horn*; Laurie Holloway, *p*; Spike Heatley, *b*; Rodney Stewart, *b*; Terry Emery, *perc*; John Dean, *perc*; Bill LeSage, *perc*; Michael Jones, *sub leader*; Sidney Sax, *leader*; John Cameron, *arr*; Vic Lewis, *cond*.

> Eleanor Rigby *-a* JC
> Strawberry Fields Forever *-a* JC

All tracks on: Nems (s) 6-63723, DJM DJSL 030, CBS Sony SONY 60118

Vic Lewis and his symphony orchestra

Thursday, 27 November 1969

Large symphony orchestra; Sidney Sax, *leader*; Vic Lewis, *cond*.

> Prokofiev-4th Symphony
>   2nd Movement (Andante)   Nems 6-64097

Vic Lewis and his symphony orchestra

November 1969

> Mahler-9th Symphony
>   4th Movement (Adagio)   Nems 6-64097
> Shostakovich-5th Symphony
>   3rd Movement (Largo)   Nems 6-64097
> Lewis-Prelude Beverly Hills *-a* KC   Nems 6-64097

The Vic Lewis orchestra and singers

1969

Large orchestra, vocal group, Ken Thorne, *arr*; Vic Lewis, *cond*.

> Come and Get It *-a* KT   Nems 56-4700, Epic 5-10580
> No Other Heart *-a* KT   Nems 56-4700, Epic 5-10580

Robin Gibb accompanied by Vic Lewis and his orchestra

1969

Large orchestra; Robin Gibb, *vcl*; Kenny Clayton, *arr*; Vic Lewis, *cond*.

> Weekend *-v* RG, *a* KC   Polydor 56368 B, 583085, Atco SD
>   33-323
> Give Me a Smile *-v* RG, *a* KC   Polydor 583085, Atco SD 33-323

Note: Other titles not conducted by Vic Lewis.

The Royal Philharmonic orchestra conducted by Vic Lewis

Friday, 8 December 1972   CTS

Large orchestra; Erich Gruenberg, *vln, leader*; Kenny Clayton, *p, arr*; Vic Lewis, *cond*.

> Sailing Homeward *-a* KC   DJM DJLPH 430, DJS 273
> Romance for Violin (WHO) *-a* KC   DJM DJLPS 437, DJS 273
> Things to Come   DJM DJLPS 437

The Royal Philharmonic orchestra conducted by Vic Lewis

27 or 28 December 1972   CTS

add Johnny Keating, *arr*

THE SHADOW OF YOUR SMILE -*a* JK, *v* EG	DJM DJLPH 430, SPECB 103

The Royal Philharmonic orchestra conducted by Vic Lewis

8 December 1972   CTS

add Ken Thorne, *arr*; John Barry, *arr*; Walter Scharf, *arr*; Johnny Scott, *arr*

LET ME DREAM -*a* KT	DJM DJLPH 430
LOVE THEME -*a* KT, *p* KC	DJM DJLPH 430
INNOCENT BYSTANDERS -*a* JK	DJM DJLPH 430
ENGLAND MADE ME -*a* JS	DJM DJLPH 430
THE ME I NEVER KNEW -*a* JB	DJM DJLPH 430
TEMPO DI AMOR -*a* JK	DJM DJLPH 430
BEN -*a* WS	DJM DJLPH 430
BROTHER SUN SISTER MOON -*a* KT	DJM DJLPH 430

The Royal Philharmonic orchestra conducted by Vic Lewis

Wednesday, 5 September 1973   CTS

Large orchestra; Erich Gruenberg, *leader*; Kenny Clayton, *p, arr*; Vic Lewis, *arr, cond.*

CONCERTO DE ARANJEUZ -*p* KC	DJM DJLPS 437, DJS 287
NONE BUT THE LONELY HEART -*a* VL, KC, *p* KC	DJM DJLPS 437
RHAPSODY ON A THEME OF PAGANINI -*p* KC	DJM DJLPS 437

The Royal Philharmonic orchestra conducted by Vic Lewis

6 September 1973   CTS

add Ken Thorne, *arr*; Johnny Keating, *arr*; Elmer Bernstein, *arr*

HOMAGE TO A PRINCESS -*a* KT	DJM DJLPS 437, DJS 287
IN TIME -*a* JK	DJM DJLPS 437
CHANSON -*a* KT	DJM DJLPS 437
BEYOND THE HILL -*a* KT	DJM DJLPS 437
HELENA -*a* EB	DJM DJLPS 437
CONCERTO NO. 2 (Andante) for piano and orchestra in F major opus 101 -*p* KC	DJM DJLPS 437

The Royal Philharmonic orchestra conducted by Vic Lewis

22 October 1974   CTS

Principal musicians: James Watson, *tp*; David Lee, *frh*; David Strange, *cello*; Erich Gruenberg, *vln, leader*; Frederick Riddle, *viola*; Derek Wickens, *oboe*; Susan Milan, *fl*; Kenny Clayton, *p, arr*; Unknown vocal group; Henry Mancini, *arr*; Allyn Ferguson, *arr*; Ken Thorne, *arr*; Nelson Riddle, *arr*; Vic Lewis, *arr, cond.*

MOON RIVER -*a* HM	Pye NSPH 401, PRT CD MP 8827
THE FOLKS WHO LIVE ON THE HILL -*a* KC, *fl* SM	Pye NSPH 401, PRT CD MP 8827
BY THE TIME I GET TO PHOENIX -*a* KC	Pye NSPH 401, PRT CD MP 8827
THIS IS ALL I ASK -*a* AF, *v* EG	Pye NSPH 401, PRT CD MP 8827
MISTY -*a* KC, *p* KC	Pye NSPH 401, PRT CD MP 8827
ALFIE -*a* AF	Pye NSPH 401, PRT CD MP 8827
SOMETHING -*a* KC	Pye NSPH 401, PRT CD MP 8827
HAVE I CHANGED -*a* AF, *v* EG	Pye NSPH 401, PRT CD MP 8827
UNFORGETTABLE -*a* NR	Pye NSPH 401, PRT CD MP 8827
BORN FREE -*a* KC	Pye NSPH 401, PRT CD MP 8827
YOUR SONG -*v* VG, *a* KT	Pye NSPH 401, PRT CD MP 8827
THE LONG AND WINDING ROAD -*v* VG, *a* KT	Pye NSPH 401, PRT CD MP 8827

The Royal Philharmonic orchestra conducted by Vic Lewis

27 Oct 1974   CTS

Same principal musicians as 74-01 plus Ashley Arbuckle, *vln*; Prudence Whittaker, *cl*; Ken Thorne, *arr*; Johnny Keating, *arr*; Vic Lewis, *cond.*

WHAT A WONDERFUL WORLD -*a* KT	Pye NSPH 402, PRT CD MP 8821
TAKE FIVE -*a* KT	Pye NSPH 402, PRT CD MP 8821

I've Got it Bad and that Ain't Good -*a* JK,   Pye NSPH 402, PRT CD MP 8821
  viola FR
Artistry in Kenton -*a* JK, *v* EG   Pye NSPH 402, PRT CD MP 8821
A Balade -*a* KT   Pye NSPH 402, PRT CD MP 8821
Moonlight Serenade -*a* JK, *cello* DS   Pye NSPH 402, PRT CD MP 8821
Embraceable You -*a* KT   Pye NSPH 402, PRT CD MP 8821
Lullaby of Birdland (fugue) -*a* JK   Pye NSPH 402, PRT CD MP 8821
Laura -*a* KT   Pye NSPH 402, PRT CD MP 8821
Where or When -*a* JK, *vln* AA   Pye NSPH 402, PRT CD MP 8821
Romeo and Juliet (finale)   Pye NSPH 402, PRT CD MP 8821

The Royal Philharmonic orchestra conducted by Vic Lewis

Tuesday, 23 September 1975   24+27 / 11 /75   CTS

Featured principals and soloists James Watson, *tp*; Derek Wickens, *oboe*; Susan Milan, *fl*; David Strange, *cello*; Joan Brown, *singer*; Erich Gruenberg, *leader*; Ken Thorne, *arr*; Vic Lewis, *cond*.

  Medley 1   Pye NSPL 41510, PRT CD MSP 7780
  Lawrence of Arabia
  Chim Chim Cheree
  Butch Cassidy and the Sundance Kid
  Dr Zhivago
  Let It Be
  Shaft -*a* KT

The Royal Philharmonic orchestra and chorus conducted by Vic Lewis

September 1975   24 + 27 /11 /75   CTS

add Allyn Ferguson, *arr*

  Lapis Lazuli -*a* KT   Pye NSPL 41510, PRT CD MSP 7780
        Pye NSPL 41510
  If Ever I Should Leave You -*a* AF   Pye NSPL 41510
  My Love -*a* KT   Pye NSPL 41510
  Here Comes That Rainy Day -*a* AF   Pye NSPL 41510
  Medley 2
  Charade
  Bridge Over Troubled Water
  Something Coming
  The Way We Were
  MacArthur Park -*a* KT

Diane Solomon with members of the Royal Philharmonic orchestra conducted by Vic Lewis

1976   13-14/2/76   CTS

Large orchestra; Diane Solomon, *vcl*; Vic Lewis, *cond*; Ed Welch, *arr*; Bobby Patrick, *arr*.

  The Way We Were -*v* DS, *a* EW   EMI EMC 3127
  Miss You Night -*v* DS, *a* EW   EMI EMC 3127
  His House and Me -*v* DS, *a* EW   EMI EMC 3127
  Make the Most of Every Morning -*v* DS, *a* BP   EMI EMC 3127
  Last Letter -*v* DS, *a* BP   EMI EMC 3127
  Our Last Song Together -*v* DS, *a* EW   EMI EMC 3127

Note: Other titles on the above LP do not include Vic Lewis.

The Royal Philharmonic ensemble conducted by Vic Lewis

6 May, 7 May 1976   CTS

Erich Gruenberg, *vln, leader*; Ashley Arbuckle, *vln, co-leader*; Michael Cookson, *viola*; David Strange, *cello*; Eldon Fox, *cello*; Bruce Mollison, *b*; Peter Lloyds, *fl*; Derek Wickens, *oboe*; John Bimson, *frh*; Skaila Kanga, *horn*; Richard Holmes, *p*; Roland Harker, *g*; Dave Richmond, *b*; Brian Hodges, *b*; Ronnie Verrall, *d*; Joanne Brown, *singer*; Ken Thorne, *arr*; Angela Morley, *arr*; Allyn Ferguson, *arr*; Stan Meyers, *arr*; Nelson Riddle, *arr*; Bobby Patrick, *arr*; Vic Lewis, *elp* (on -*g* only), *cond*.

  Theme from Emmanuelle 2 -*a* KT, *cello* DS   EMI EMC 3173
  She Danced with Me -*a* AM   EMI EMC 3173

MY SPECIAL FRIEND -*v* JB, *a* KT	EMI EMC 3173
SOME DAY MY PRINCE WILL COME -*a* AF	EMI EMC 3173
CAVATINA -*a* SM	EMI EMC 3173
THEME FROM ROUTE 66 -*a* NR	EMI EMC 3173
EXPRESSIONS -*a* BP	EMI EMC 3173
PIECES OF DREAM -*a* KT	EMI EMC 3173
PICTURES IN A ROOM -*a* KT	EMI EMC 3173
WHEN YOU WISH UPON A STAR -*a* AF	EMI EMC 3173
ALL THE WISHING IN THE WORLD -*a* SM	EMI EMC 3173
GABRIELLE -*a* NR	EMI EMC 3173

The Royal Philharmonic orchestra conducted by Vic Lewis

December 1976   CTS

Featured soloists: James Watson, *tp*; Derek Wickens, *oboe*; Susan Milan, *fl*; David Strange, *cello*; Richard Holmes, *p*; Ashley Arbuckle, *co-leader*; Barry Griffiths, *leader*; Ken Thorne, *arr*; Allyn Ferguson, *arr*; Vic Lewis, *cond*.

DON'T CRY FOR ME ARGENTINA -*a* KT	RCA PL 25043, RCA 2772
THEME FROM MASH -*a* KT	RCA PL 25043
SERENADE FOR STRINGS -*a* KT	RCA PL 25043, RCA 2772
COCO/ALWAYS MADEMOISELLE -*a* KT	RCA PL 25043
HANNIE CAULDER -*a* KT	RCA PL 25043
49TH PARALLEL	RCA PL 25043
SO MUCH YOU LOVED ME -*a* KT	RCA PL 25043
LOUISE -*a* AF	RCA PL 25043
ESCAPE ME NEVER	RCA PL 25043
MY SHIP -*a* AF	RCA PL 25043
LITTLE PRINCE -*a* KT	RCA PL 25043

The Royal Philharmonic orchestra conducted by Vic Lewis

October 1977   CTS

Featured soloists: Ray Simmonds, *tp*; Jeffrey Bryany, *frh*; Derek Wickens, *oboe*; Susan Milan, *fl*; Prudence Whittaker, *cl*; Michael Cookson, *viola*; Fiona Hibbert, *horn*; Barry Griffiths, *leader*; Ken Thorne, *arr*; Vic Lewis, *cond*.

OCHRE	RCA PL 25123
RED	RCA PL 25123
GREEN	RCA PL 25123
SIENNA	RCA PL 25123
BLACK	RCA PL 25123
MAUVE	RCA PL 25123
GOLD	RCA PL 25123
AZURE	RCA PL 25123
YELLOW	RCA PL 25123
GREY	RCA PL 25123

Shorty Rogers/Bud Shank quintet

Concorde Club, Southampton, Wednesday, 2 May 1984
Shorty Rogers, *flh*; Bud Shank, *fl*, *as*; Vic Lewis, *p*; Ron Matthewson, *b*; Kenny Clare, *d*.

| BACK AGAIN | Concept VL-1 |

John Critchenson, *p*, replaces Lewis.

LIFT OFF	Concept VL-1, Choice 6829
WARM VALLEY	Concept VL-1, Choice 6829
MY ROMANCE	Concept VL-1, Choice 6829

Vic Lewis and his big band featuring Shorty Rogers and Bud Shank

Wembley, Tuesday, 8 May 1984
Simon Gardner, *tp*; Mike O'Gorman, *tp*; Steve Sidwell, *tp*; David Plews, *tp*; Paul Spong, *tp*; Shorty Rogers, *flh*; Faez Virji (*tb*); Neil Sidwell, *tb*; Richard Edwards, *tb*; Nick Gallant, *btb*; Ronnie Chamberlain, *fl*, *as*; Cliff Tracey, *fl*, *as*; Dave Bishop, *fl*, *ts*; Jamie Talbot, *fl*, *ts*, *bs*; Bob McKay, *bcl*, *bs*; John Critchenson, *p*; Ron Matthewson, *b*; Kenny Clare, *d*; Bill Holman, *arr*; Vic Lewis, *dir*.

| SHORTY | Concept VL-1, Choice 6829 |

add Bud Shank, *fl*, *as*; Jane Hanna, *frh*. Shorty Rogers does not play but composed and arranged track *-b*.

    BUD SHANK   Concept VL-1, Choice 6829
        (a) DEEP ROOTS (1950)
        (b) DOWN HOME (1963)
        (c) EVOLVING (1984)
        (d) FULL CIRCLE

Vic Lewis and the BBC radio big band

Thursday, 12 September 1985

Nigel Carter, *tp*; Brian Rankine, *tp*; Paul Eshelby, *tp*; Bill Turner, *tp*; Jiggs Whigham, *tb*; Colin Sheen, *tb*; Gordon Campbell, *tb*; Eddie Lorkin, *tb*; Andrew Fawbert, *tb*; Bud Shank, *fl*, *as*; Barry Robinson, *fl*, *cl*, *as*; Gordon Keates, *fl*, *cl*, *as*; Peter King, *as*; Peter Warner, *fl*, *cl*, *ts*; Nigel Nash, *cl*, *bass cl*, *ts*; Derek Hyams, *cl*, *as*, *bs*; Andrew Vinter, *p*; Graham Atha, *g*; Len Walker, *g*; Roy Babbington, *b*; Ronnie Verrall, *d*; John Chambers, *perc*; Barry Forgie, *arr*; Bill Holman, *arr*; Gerry Mulligan, *arr*; Shorty Rogers, *arr*; Allyn Ferguson, *arr*; Ken Thorne, *arr*; John Cameron, *arr*; Vic Lewis, *dir*, *cond*.

INTERMISSION RIFF *-a* BF, *fl* BS, *as* PK, *tb* JW	Concept VL 3
LOVERMAN *-a* BH, *as* BS	Concept VL 3
APPLE PIE *-a* GM, *as* BS, *tb* JW, *as* PK	Concept VL 3
CONVERSATION *-a* SR, *tb* JW, *as* PK	Concept VL 3
TRIPLE THREAT *-a* AF, *tb* JW, *as* BS, *as* PK	Concept VL 3
SUNDAY GIRL *-a* KT, *as* BS, *tb* JW	Concept VL 3
THE LONELIEST MONK *-a* JC, *as* BS, *tb* JW, *as* PK	Concept VL 3
GO LITELEY *-a* BH, *as* BS, *tb* JW, *as* PK	Concept VL 3

Index